Birth Control

Other Books in the Issues on Trial Series:

Birth Control

Noël Merino, Book Editor

GREENHAVEN PRESS
A part of Gale, Cengage Learning

GALE
CENGAGE Learning·

Detroit • New York • San Francisco • New Haven, Conn • Waterville, Maine • London

GALE
CENGAGE Learning

Christine Nasso, *Publisher*
Elizabeth Des Chenes, *Managing Editor*

© 2011 Greenhaven Press, a part of Gale, Cengage Learning

For more information, contact:
Greenhaven Press
27500 Drake Rd.
Farmington Hills, MI 48331-3535
Or you can visit our Internet site at gale.cengage.com.

For product information and technology assistance, contact us at

Gale Customer Support, 1-800-877-4253
For permission to use material from this text or product, submit all requests online at
www.cengage.com/permissions
Further permissions questions can be emailed to permissionrequest@cengage.com

Articles in Greenhaven Press anthologies are often edited for length to meet page requirements. In addition, original titles of these works are changed to clearly present the main thesis and to explicitly indicate the author's opinion. Every effort is made to ensure that Greenhaven Press accurately reflects the original intent of the authors. Every effort has been made to trace the owners of copyrighted material.

Cover Image © Bettmann/Corbis.

LIBRARY OF CONGRESS CATALOGING-IN-PUBLICATION DATA

Birth control / Noël Merino, book editor.
    p. cm. -- (Issues on trial)
    Includes bibliographical references and index.
    ISBN 978-0-7377-4947-2 (hardcover)
    1. Birth control--Juvenile literature. 2. Birth control--Law and legislation--
Juvenile literature. I. Merino, Noël.
    HQ766.B478 2010
    344.7304'8--dc22
                                                         2010019295

Printed in the United States of America
1 2 3 4 5 6 7 14 13 12 11 10

Contents

Chapter 1: Laws Banning Birth Control for Married Persons Are Unconstitutional

   In *Griswold v. Connecticut*, the Supreme Court overturned the convictions of two people found guilty of violating a Connecticut law prohibiting the use of any contraceptive device, determining that such a law violates the intent of several constitutional amendments to guarantee privacy.

   In his dissenting opinion, Black, although finding the Connecticut law offensive, finds nothing in the Constitution that prohibits state legislatures from passing laws that prevent married couples from using contraception.

   A scholar argues that the right to privacy identified in *Griswold*, which created the foundation for the reproductive rights of women, is currently threatened by even a small conservative change in the Supreme Court.

   A commentator argues that there is no general right to privacy in the U.S. Constitution and that, as a consequence, the decisions in *Griswold* and later cases were incorrect.

A law professor argues that the right to privacy in reproductive issues identified in *Eisenstadt* applies to men as well as to women, and needs to be given greater legal weight than it currently is given.

A lawyer contends that the *Eisenstadt* ruling supports the rights of gays and lesbians to have children, and she believes that homosexuals should be free from discrimination with respect to legal issues pertaining to marriage and children.

Chapter 3: Laws Banning Abortion Are Unconstitutional

In *Roe v. Wade*, the Supreme Court determined that the right to privacy protected the decision by women of whether or not to have an abortion.

In his dissenting opinion, Rehnquist finds nothing in the U.S. Constitution that protects the right to have an abortion or that prevents states from having laws restricting abortion.

A policy analyst contends that state policies aimed at making it harder to get an abortion have not had a significant impact on pregnant women's choices.

Chapter 4: Laws Banning Birth Control for Minors Are Unconstitutional

An attorney contends that parents have the right to raise their children as they see fit and that their current rights under the law need to be expanded, as they have been since the Court's decision in *Carey.*

Foreword

The U.S. courts have long served as a battleground for the most highly charged and contentious issues of the time. Divisive matters are often brought into the legal system by activists who feel strongly for their cause and demand an official resolution. Indeed, subjects that give rise to intense emotions or involve closely held religious or moral beliefs lay at the heart of the most polemical court rulings in history. One such case was *Brown v. Board of Education* (1954), which ended racial segregation in schools. Prior to *Brown*, the courts had held that blacks could be forced to use separate facilities as long as these facilities were equal to that of whites.

For years many groups had opposed segregation based on religious, moral, and legal grounds. Educators produced heartfelt testimony that segregated schooling greatly disadvantaged black children. They noted that in comparison to whites, blacks received a substandard education in deplorable conditions. Religious leaders such as Martin Luther King Jr. preached that the harsh treatment of blacks was immoral and unjust. Many involved in civil rights law, such as Thurgood Marshall, called for equal protection of all people under the law, as their study of the Constitution had indicated that segregation was illegal and un-American. Whatever their motivation for ending the practice, and despite the threats they received from segregationists, these ardent activists remained unwavering in their cause.

Those fighting against the integration of schools were mainly white southerners who did not believe that whites and blacks should intermingle. Blacks were subordinate to whites, they maintained, and society had to resist any attempt to break down strict color lines. Some white southerners charged that segregated schooling was *not* hindering blacks' education. For example, Virginia attorney general J. Lindsay Almond asserted, "With the help and the sympathy and the love and respect of the white people of the South, the colored man has risen under that educational process to a place of eminence and respect throughout the nation. It has served him well." So when the Supreme Court ruled against the segregationists in *Brown*, the South responded with vociferous cries of protest. Even government leaders criticized the decision. The governor of Arkansas, Orval Faubus, stated that he would not "be a party to any attempt to force acceptance of change to which the people are so overwhelmingly opposed." Indeed, resistance to integration was so great that when black students arrived at the formerly all-white Central High School in Arkansas, federal troops had to be dispatched to quell a threatening mob of protesters.

Nevertheless, the *Brown* decision was enforced and the South integrated its schools. In this instance, the Court, while not settling the issue to everyone's satisfaction, functioned as an instrument of progress by forcing a major social change. Historian David Halberstam observes that the *Brown* ruling "deprived segregationist practices of their moral legitimacy. . . . It was therefore perhaps the single most important moment of the decade, the moment that separated the old order from the new and helped create the tumultuous era just arriving." Considered one of the most important victories for civil rights, *Brown* paved the way for challenges to racial segregation in many areas, including on public buses and in restaurants.

In examining *Brown*, it becomes apparent that the courts play an influential role—and face an arduous challenge—in shaping the debate over emotionally charged social issues. Judges must balance competing interests, keeping in mind the high stakes and intense emotions on both sides. As exemplified by *Brown*, judicial decisions often upset the status quo and initiate significant changes in society. Greenhaven Press's Issues on Trial series captures the controversy surrounding influential court rulings and explores the social ramifications of such decisions from varying perspectives. Each anthology highlights one social issue—such as the death penalty, students' rights, or wartime civil liberties. Each volume then focuses on key historical and contemporary court cases that helped mold the issue as we know it today. The books include a compendium of primary sources—court rulings, dissents, and immediate reactions to the rulings—as well as secondary sources from experts in the field, people involved in the cases, legal analysts, and other commentators opining on the implications and legacy of the chosen cases. An annotated table of contents, an in-depth introduction, and prefaces that overview each case all provide context as readers delve into the topic at hand. To help students fully probe the subject, each volume contains book and periodical bibliographies, a comprehensive index, and a list of organizations to contact. With these features, the Issues on Trial series offers a well-rounded perspective on the courts' role in framing society's thorniest, most impassioned debates.

Introduction

In the early part of American history, the Christian majority considered birth control—the use of contraceptives—immoral. In the mid-nineteenth century, several states passed laws banning the distribution and use of contraceptives. In 1873 Congress passed An Act of the Suppression of Trade in, and Circulation of, Obscene Literature and Articles of Immoral Use, more commonly known as the Comstock Act. This act originally prohibited the use of contraceptives in the District of Columbia and other areas of federal jurisdiction, as well as prohibiting the use of the U.S. postal service for sending such devices. It later criminalized shipments of contraceptives across state lines. Margaret Sanger, a birth control activist and the founder of the American Birth Control League, was a leader among the many who fought for the lifting of restrictions on birth control, but it was not until 1965—just months before Sanger's death—that the U.S. Supreme Court would first begin to pave the way for greater reproductive freedom for Americans. Underlying all major Court decisions on birth control, which struck down laws that had a long history in the United States, was the recognition of the controversial right of privacy.

The Right of Privacy

After many years of refusing to hear appeals on the issue of laws prohibiting contraceptives, the Court heard the case of *Griswold v. Connecticut* (1965). The case was instrumental in laying the groundwork for several future cases involving contraceptive use because of its determination that the U.S. Constitution guaranteed an implicit right of privacy. In its decision on *Griswold*, the Court struck down a Connecticut law that prohibited the use of birth control, finding that it violated the constitutional right of privacy. The decision, penned by William O. Douglas, focused not so much on a broad right of privacy as on the specific right to marital privacy. Douglas wrote that marriage was a relationship that fell within constitutionally protected "zones of privacy." Those zones are not explicitly mentioned in the Constitution, but Douglas wrote that the right to marital privacy was implicitly guaranteed by several parts of the Constitution, including the First, Third, Fifth, Ninth, and Fourteenth Amendments, calling the right of privacy in marriage "older than the Bill of Rights."

The right to marital privacy identified in *Griswold* formed the basis for a variety of other decisions that led to the lifting of restrictions on the distribution and use of birth control. In *Eisenstadt v. Baird* (1972), the Court ruled that a Massachusetts law prohibiting the sale or distribution of contraceptives to unmarried persons violated the equal protection clause of the Fourteenth Amendment. The Court reasoned that there was no good justification for treating married and unmarried persons differently with respect to the right to privacy in matters of reproduction, thus extending the same birth control freedoms identified in *Griswold* to unmarried persons. Later, in *Carey v. Population Services International* (1977), the Court extended the freedom to use contraceptives to minors, thereby extending the right to privacy in matters of reproduction to all people, regardless of their marital status or age.

The Controversial Cases

Many of the birth control cases decided by the Supreme Court were controversial, at least at the time of the ruling. By far the most controversial case regarding birth control to stem from the *Griswold* decision is *Roe v. Wade* (1973). In *Roe*, the Court found that the right of privacy was "broad enough to encompass a woman's decision whether or not to terminate her pregnancy." By the time of the *Roe* decision, the right of privacy had been cited in many cases, and the Court noted that its own past decisions supported the right of privacy with respect to activities related to "marriage, procreation, contraception, family relationships, and childrearing and education." The Court determined that these past decisions, known in legal circles as precedent, supported a woman's right to have an abortion with few restrictions in early pregnancy. The Court continues to hear cases on restrictions related to abortion, though it has continued to reiterate the central holding of *Roe*, finding the right of privacy to support a woman's right to have an abortion.

The Supreme Court cases on birth control are controversial not just for the content of their rulings but also for how this line of jurisprudence has been used in other areas of the law. The right of privacy developed through this line of cases was cited in *Lawrence v. Texas* (2003), wherein the Court struck down state laws that criminalized homosexual sodomy. In its decision, the Court cited its previous decisions in *Griswold, Eisenstadt, Roe, Carey,* and others as supporting the unconstitutionality of laws that criminalize homosexual acts between consenting adults.

While many of the Supreme Court's decisions based on the right of privacy are controversial, it is not clear that any of them can be reversed without a reversal of the entire line of precedent that rests upon the right of privacy. Within the Court's rulings on birth control, this means that a reversal of *Roe* could mean reversals on birth control decisions all the way back to *Griswold*. Some would argue, however, that whereas the right to privacy may protect the use of condoms by married persons, it does not extend all the way to a woman's right to choose abortion.

The debate about the right of privacy first identified by the Court in *Griswold* and the ensuing Court decisions is likely one that will not end anytime soon. This anthology seeks to explore this debate by examining four major Court decisions relating to birth control in America: *Griswold v. Connecticut* (1965), *Eisenstadt v. Baird* (1972), *Roe v. Wade*

(1973), and *Carey v. Population Services International* (1977). By presenting the Supreme Court's decisions, the views of dissenting justices, and commentary on the impact of the cases, *Issues on Trial: Birth Control* sheds light on how the legal understanding of birth control—as well as the right to privacy—in the United States has evolved and continues to evolve.

CHAPTER 1

Laws Banning Birth Control for Married Persons Are Unconstitutional

Case Overview

Griswold v. Connecticut (1965)

Griswold v. Connecticut involved an 1879 Connecticut law that made it illegal for anyone to counsel on the subject of contraception or to prescribe contraception to married people. The law stated, "any person who uses any drug, medicinal article or instrument for the purpose of preventing conception shall be fined not less than fifty dollars or imprisoned not less than sixty days," while also noting that "any person who assists, abets, counsels, causes, hires or commands another to commit any offense may be prosecuted and punished as if he were the principal offender." The law had not been enforced for decades, and doctors had regularly provided contraception to married couples and faced no legal penalty. The executive director of the Planned Parenthood League of Connecticut, Estelle Griswold, and its medical director, Lee Buxton, a physician and professor at Yale University School of Medicine, were convicted under the law for distributing contraception to married couples and fined $100 each. They appealed to the Supreme Court of Errors of Connecticut, which upheld their conviction. They then appealed their case to the U.S. Supreme Court, claiming that the law was unconstitutional.

The Supreme Court reversed the lower court rulings, finding that there was a right to privacy protecting reproductive decisions within marriage, even though there is no explicit right to privacy mentioned in the Constitution. Writing for the majority, William O. Douglas argued that there are "penumbras," or shady areas, to the Bill of Rights—specifically, the penumbras of the First, Third, Fifth, Ninth, and Fourteenth Amendments—that create "zones of privacy" that may not be violated. In particular, the Court noted, the marital relationship lies "within the zone of privacy created by several fundamental constitutional guarantees." The Court concluded that any law, such as Connecticut's, that violates marital privacy is unconstitutional.

In subsequent Supreme Court rulings, the right to privacy first identified in *Griswold* was expanded into areas outside of marriage. The cases are discussed in the other chapters of this book. The Court's decision in *Griswold* is to this day hotly debated due to the fact that a right to privacy is never explicitly mentioned in the U.S. Constitution.

> "We deal [in this case] with a right of
> privacy older than the Bill of Rights—
> older than our political parties, older
> than our school system."

Majority Opinion:
The Right to Privacy Protects
Marital Use of Contraceptives

William O. Douglas

*William O. Douglas was appointed to the U.S. Supreme Court
by President Franklin D. Roosevelt in 1939. Serving for more
than thirty-six years, he holds the record for the longest continu-
ous service on the Court.*

*The following is the majority opinion in the 1965 case of
Griswold v. Connecticut, the Supreme Court ruling that reversed a lower court's decision convicting two individuals from a
medical center for violating a Connecticut law that forbade any
person from assisting another in getting birth control. The two
individuals had counseled only married people about contraception. Writing for the Court, Douglas found that the Connecticut
law violated the right to privacy—implicit in the penumbras, or
implications, of the First, Third, Fourth, Fifth, and Ninth
Amendments of the U.S. Constitution.*

Appellant Griswold is Executive Director of the Planned
Parenthood League of Connecticut. Appellant Buxton is a
licensed physician and a professor at the Yale Medical School
who served as Medical Director for the League at its Center in

William O. Douglas, majority opinion, *Griswold v. Connecticut*, U.S. Supreme Court,
June 7, 1965.

New Haven—a center open and operating from November 1 to November 10, 1961, when appellants were arrested.

They gave information, instruction, and medical advice to *married persons* as to the means of preventing conception. They examined the wife and prescribed the best contraceptive device or material for her use. Fees were usually charged, although some couples were serviced free.

Laws Against Contraception

The statutes whose constitutionality is involved in this appeal are §§ 53-32 and 54-196 of the General Statutes of Connecticut (1958 rev.). The former provides:

> Any person who uses any drug, medicinal article or instrument for the purpose of preventing conception shall be fined not less than fifty dollars or imprisoned not less than sixty days nor more than one year or be both fined and imprisoned.

Section 54-196 provides:

> Any person who assists, abets, counsels, causes, hires or commands another to commit any offense may be prosecuted and punished as if he were the principal offender.

The appellants were found guilty as accessories and fined $100 each, against the claim that the accessory statute, as so applied, violated the Fourteenth Amendment. The Appellate Division of the Circuit Court affirmed. The Supreme Court of Errors affirmed that judgment. We noted probable jurisdiction.

We think that appellants have standing to raise the constitutional rights of the married people with whom they had a professional relationship. . . .

The rights of husband and wife, pressed here, are likely to be diluted or adversely affected unless those rights are considered in a suit involving those who have this kind of confidential relation to them.

The First and Fourteenth Amendments

Coming to the merits, we are met with a wide range of questions that implicate the Due Process Clause of the Fourteenth Amendment. . . . We do not sit as a super-legislature to determine the wisdom, need, and propriety of laws that touch economic problems, business affairs, or social conditions. This law, however, operates directly on an intimate relation of husband and wife and their physician's role in one aspect of that relation.

The association of people is not mentioned in the Constitution nor in the Bill of Rights. The right to educate a child in a school of the parents' choice—whether public or private or parochial—is also not mentioned. Nor is the right to study any particular subject or any foreign language. Yet the First Amendment has been construed to include certain of those rights.

By *Pierce v. Society of Sisters* [1925], the right to educate one's children as one chooses is made applicable to the States by the force of the First and Fourteenth Amendments. By *Meyer v. Nebraska* [1923], the same dignity is given the right to study the German language in a private school. In other words, the State may not, consistently with the spirit of the First Amendment, contract the spectrum of available knowledge. The right of freedom of speech and press includes not only the right to utter or to print, but the right to distribute, the right to receive, the right to read and freedom of inquiry, freedom of thought, and freedom to teach—indeed, the freedom of the entire university community. Without those peripheral rights, the specific rights would be less secure. And so we reaffirm the principle of the *Pierce* and the *Meyer* cases.

In *NAACP v. Alabama* [1958], we protected the "freedom to associate and privacy in one's associations," noting that freedom of association was a peripheral First Amendment right. Disclosure of membership lists of a constitutionally valid association, we held, was invalid as entailing the likelihood of a substantial restraint upon the exercise by petitioner's members of their right to freedom of association.

In other words, the First Amendment has a penumbra where privacy is protected from governmental intrusion. In like context, we have protected forms of "association" that are not political in the customary sense, but pertain to the social, legal, and economic benefit of the members. In *Schware v. Board of Bar Examiners* [1957], we held it not permissible to bar a lawyer from practice because he had once been a member of the Communist Party. The man's "association with that Party" was not shown to be "anything more than a political faith in a political party," and was not action of a kind proving bad moral character.

Those cases involved more than the "right of assembly"—a right that extends to all, irrespective of their race or ideology. The right of "association," like the right of belief, is more than the right to attend a meeting; it includes the right to express one's attitudes or philosophies by membership in a group or by affiliation with it or by other lawful means. Association in that context is a form of expression of opinion, and, while it is not expressly included in the First Amendment, its existence is necessary in making the express guarantees fully meaningful.

Penumbras of Amendments

The foregoing cases suggest that specific guarantees in the Bill of Rights have penumbras, formed by emanations from those guarantees that help give them life and substance. Various guarantees create zones of privacy. The right of association contained in the penumbra of the First Amendment is one, as we have seen. The Third Amendment, in its prohibition against the quartering of soldiers "in any house" in time of peace without the consent of the owner, is another facet of that privacy. The Fourth Amendment explicitly affirms the "right of the people to be secure in their persons, houses, papers, and effects, against unreasonable searches and seizures." The Fifth Amendment, in its Self-Incrimination Clause, enables the citizen to create a zone of privacy which government may not force him to surrender to his detriment. The Ninth Amendment provides: "The enumeration in the Constitution, of certain rights, shall not be construed to deny or disparage others retained by the people."

The Fourth and Fifth Amendments were described in *Boyd v. United States* [1886], as protection against all governmental invasions "of the sanctity of a man's home and the privacies of life." We recently referred in *Mapp v. Ohio* [1961], to the Fourth Amendment as creating a "right to privacy, no less important than any other right carefully and particularly reserved to the people."

We have had many controversies over these penumbral rights of "privacy and repose." These cases bear witness that the right of privacy which presses for recognition here is a legitimate one.

The Right of Privacy in Marriage

The present case, then, concerns a relationship lying within the zone of privacy created by several fundamental constitutional guarantees. And it concerns a law which, in forbidding the use of contraceptives, rather than regulating their manufacture or sale, seeks to achieve its goals by means having a maximum destructive impact upon that relationship. Such a law cannot stand in light of the familiar principle, so often applied by this Court, that a

> governmental purpose to control or prevent activities constitutionally subject to state regulation may not be achieved by means which sweep unnecessarily broadly and thereby invade the area of protected freedoms. [*NAACP v. Alabama.*]

Would we allow the police to search the sacred precincts of marital bedrooms for telltale signs of the use of contraceptives? The very idea is repulsive to the notions of privacy surrounding the marriage relationship.

We deal with a right of privacy older than the Bill of Rights—older than our political parties, older than our school system. Marriage is a coming together for better or for worse, hopefully enduring, and intimate to the degree of being sacred. It is an association that promotes a way of life, not causes; a harmony in living, not political faiths; a bilateral loyalty, not commercial or social projects. Yet it is an association for as noble a purpose as any involved in our prior decisions.

> "The Court talks about a constitutional 'right of privacy' as though there is some constitutional provision or provisions forbidding any law ever to be passed which might abridge the 'privacy' of individuals."

Dissenting Opinion: No Constitutional Right to Privacy Exists

Hugo Black

Hugo Black was one of President Franklin D. Roosevelt's nominees to the U.S. Supreme Court and served from 1937 to 1971. He is known for advocating a literal reading of the U.S. Constitution.

In the following excerpt from Black's dissent in the 1965 case of Griswold v. Connecticut, *Black claims that there is no basis for finding Connecticut's law criminalizing the use of contraceptives unconstitutional. Though Black admits he does not like the law, he claims that the Supreme Court does not have the right to strike down any state law it finds repugnant. Rather, Black takes a strictly literal view of the Constitution and believes the Court should only find laws unconstitutional when it is explicitly mandated by the Constitution. He does not believe that there is any broad right to privacy guaranteed by the U.S. Constitution.*

I do not to any extent whatever base my view that this Connecticut law is constitutional on a belief that the law is wise, or that its policy is a good one. In order that there may

Hugo Black, dissenting opinion, *Griswold v. Connecticut*, U.S. Supreme Court, June 7, 1965.

be no room at all to doubt why I vote as I do, I feel constrained to add that the law is every bit as offensive to me as it is to my Brethren of the majority and my Brothers [John Marshall] Harlan, [Byron] White and [Arthur] Goldberg, who, reciting reasons why it is offensive to them, hold it unconstitutional. There is no single one of the graphic and eloquent strictures and criticisms fired at the policy of this Connecticut law either by the Court's opinion or by those of my concurring Brethren to which I cannot subscribe—except their conclusion that the evil qualities they see in the law make it unconstitutional.

The Scope of the First Amendment

Had the doctor defendant here, or even the nondoctor defendant, been convicted for doing nothing more than expressing opinions to persons coming to the clinic that certain contraceptive devices, medicines or practices would do them good and would be desirable, or for telling people how devices could be used, I can think of no reasons at this time why their expressions of views would not be protected by the First and Fourteenth Amendments, which guarantee freedom of speech. But speech is one thing; conduct and physical activities are quite another. The two defendants here were active participants in an organization which gave physical examinations to women, advised them what kind of contraceptive devices or medicines would most likely be satisfactory for them, and then supplied the devices themselves, all for a graduated scale of fees, based on the family income. Thus, these defendants admittedly engaged with others in a planned course of conduct to help people violate the Connecticut law. Merely because some speech was used in carrying on that conduct—just as, in ordinary life, some speech accompanies most kinds of conduct—we are not, in my view, justified in holding that the First Amendment forbids the State to punish their conduct. Strongly as I desire to protect all First Amendment freedoms,

I am unable to stretch the Amendment so as to afford protection to the conduct of these defendants in violating the Connecticut law. What would be the constitutional fate of the law if hereafter applied to punish nothing but speech is, as I have said, quite another matter. The Court talks about a constitutional "right of privacy" as though there is some constitutional provision or provisions forbidding any law ever to be passed which might abridge the "privacy" of individuals. But there is not. There are, of course, guarantees in certain specific constitutional provisions which are designed in part to protect privacy at certain times and places with respect to certain activities. Such, for example, is the Fourth Amendment's guarantee against "unreasonable searches and seizures." But I think it belittles that Amendment to talk about it as though it protects nothing but "privacy." To treat it that way is to give it a niggardly [narrow or stingy] interpretation, not the kind of liberal reading I think any Bill of Rights provision should be given. The average man would very likely not have his feelings soothed any more by having his property seized openly than by having it seized privately and by stealth. He simply wants his property left alone. And a person can be just as much, if not more, irritated, annoyed and injured by an unceremonious public arrest by a policeman as he is by a seizure in the privacy of his office or home.

One of the most effective ways of diluting or expanding a constitutionally guaranteed right is to substitute for the crucial word or words of a constitutional guarantee another word or words, more or less flexible and more or less restricted in meaning. This fact is well illustrated by the use of the term "right of privacy" as a comprehensive substitute for the Fourth Amendment's guarantee against "unreasonable searches and seizures." "Privacy" is a broad, abstract and ambiguous concept which can easily be shrunken in meaning but which can also, on the other hand, easily be interpreted as a constitutional ban against many things other than searches and seizures. I have expressed the view many times that First Amendment freedoms, for example, have suffered from a failure of the courts to stick to the simple language of the First Amendment in construing it, instead of invoking multitudes of words substituted for those the Framers used. For these reasons, I get nowhere in this case by talk about a constitutional "right of privacy" as an emanation from one or more constitutional provisions. I like my privacy as well as the next one, but I am nevertheless compelled to admit that government has a right to invade it unless prohibited by some specific constitutional provision. For these reasons, I cannot agree with the Court's judgment and the reasons it gives for holding this Connecticut law unconstitutional. . . .

The Court Must Exercise Restraint

I repeat, so as not to be misunderstood, that this Court does have power, which it should exercise, to hold laws unconstitutional where they are forbidden by the Federal Constitution. My point is that there is no provision of the Constitution which either expressly or impliedly vests power in this Court to sit as a supervisory agency over acts of duly constituted legislative bodies and set aside their laws because of the Court's belief that the legislative policies adopted are unreasonable, unwise, arbitrary, capricious or irrational. The adoption of such a loose, flexible, uncontrolled standard for holding laws unconstitutional, if ever it is finally achieved, will amount to a great unconstitutional shift of power to the courts which I believe and am constrained to say will be bad for the courts, and worse for the country. Subjecting federal and state laws to such an unrestrained and unrestrainable judicial control as to the wisdom of legislative enactments would, I fear, jeopardize the separation of governmental powers that the Framers set up, and, at the same time, threaten to take away much of the power of States to govern themselves which the Constitution plainly intended them to have.

I realize that many good and able men have eloquently spoken and written, sometimes in rhapsodical strains, about the duty of this Court to keep the Constitution in tune with the times. The idea is that the Constitution must be changed from time to time, and that this Court is charged with a duty to make those changes. For myself, I must, with all deference, reject that philosophy. The Constitution makers knew the need for change, and provided for it. Amendments suggested by the people's elected representatives can be submitted to the people or their selected agents for ratification. That method of change was good for our Fathers, and, being somewhat old-fashioned, I must add it is good enough for me. And so I cannot rely on the Due Process Clause or the Ninth Amendment or any mysterious and uncertain natural law concept as a reason for striking down this state law. The Due Process Clause, with an "arbitrary and capricious" or "shocking to the conscience" formula, was liberally used by this Court to strike down economic legislation in the early decades of this century, threatening, many people thought, the tranquility and stability of the Nation. That formula, based on subjective considerations of "natural justice," is no less dangerous when used to enforce this Court's views about personal rights than those about economic rights. . . .

Authority of the State Legislature

In 1798, when this Court was asked to hold another Connecticut law unconstitutional, Justice [James] Iredell said:

> [I]t has been the policy of all the *American states* which have individually framed their state constitutions since the revolution, and of the people of the *United States* when they framed the Federal Constitution, to define with precision the objects of the legislative power, and to restrain its exercise within marked and settled boundaries. If any act of Congress, or of the Legislature of a state, violates those constitutional provisions, it is unquestionably void, though I

admit that, as the authority to declare it void is of a delicate and awful nature, the Court will never resort to that authority but in a clear and urgent case. If, on the other hand, the Legislature of the Union, or the Legislature of any member of the Union, shall pass a law within the general scope of their constitutional power, the Court cannot pronounce it to be void, merely because it is, in their judgment, contrary to the principles of natural justice. The ideas of natural justice are regulated by no fixed standard: the ablest and the purest men have differed upon the subject, and all that the Court could properly say in such an event would be that the Legislature (possessed of an equal right of opinion) had passed an act which, in the opinion of the judges, was inconsistent with the abstract principles of natural justice. [*Calder v. Bull* (1798).]

I would adhere to that constitutional philosophy in passing on this Connecticut law today. I am not persuaded to deviate from the view which I stated in 1947 in *Adamson v. California*:

Since *Marbury v. Madison* [1803], was decided, the practice has been firmly established, for better or worse, that courts can strike down legislative enactments which violate the Constitution. This process, of course, involves interpretation, and since words can have many meanings, interpretation obviously may result in contraction or extension of the original purpose of a constitutional provision, thereby affecting policy. But to pass upon the constitutionality of statutes by looking to the particular standards enumerated in the Bill of Rights and other parts of the Constitution is one thing; to invalidate statutes because of application of "natural law" deemed to be above and undefined by the Constitution is another.

In the one instance, courts, proceeding within clearly marked constitutional boundaries, seek to execute policies written into the Constitution; in the other, they roam at will in the limitless area of their own beliefs as to reasonableness, and actually select policies, a responsibility which the Constitution entrusts to the legislative representatives of the people. . . .

So far as I am concerned, Connecticut's law, as applied here, is not forbidden by any provision of the Federal Constitution as that Constitution was written, and I would therefore affirm.

> *"The appointment of just one new conservative justice to the Court could threaten* all *constitutional protections for abortion—and perhaps for contraception, as well."*

The Core Privacy Protection Identified in *Griswold* Is Endangered

Ellen Chesler

Ellen Chesler is a distinguished lecturer and the director of the Eleanor Roosevelt Initiative on Women and Public Policy at Hunter College in New York City. She is the author of Woman of Valor: Margaret Sanger and the Birth Control Movement in America.

In the following viewpoint, Chesler contends that the right to privacy identified by the U.S. Supreme Court in Griswold v. Connecticut, *which was used in that case to protect access to contraception by married persons, could soon be reversed by the appointment of a conservative justice to fill a 2005 vacancy. Chesler recounts how the fight for the reproductive rights of women has been a key component of the women's rights movement. One key success of that movement, she argues, is the Supreme Court's decision in* Griswold, *which eventually led to many reproductive freedoms for women, including legal abortion. With the privacy doctrine in* Griswold *under attack in recent years, she argues, even a small change on the Supreme Court in the conservative direction threatens to undo the gains of women with respect to reproductive freedom.*

Ellen Chesler, "Public Triumphs, Private Rights," *Ms.*, vol. 15, Summer 2005, pp. 34–37.

Nestled in a grove of trees, about two-thirds of the way up the steep hillock that contains the cemetery of the old Congregational Church in historic Wethersfield, Conn., an unassuming flat headstone marks the grave of Estelle Trebert Griswold, born June 8, 1900, and laid to rest beside her husband, Richard, on August 13, 1981. Estelle is buried among dozens of kinsmen reaching back many generations, but the family name was enshrined in American history only 40 years ago, on June 7, 1965, when she prevailed in a historic ruling by the United States Supreme Court.

A Landmark Ruling

The *Griswold v. Connecticut* decision protects the right of married women to practice contraception and to secure access to legal and reliable reproductive-health services. It later provided the foundation for expanding privacy protections to encompass abortion. And those are two of the critical protections now endangered by the potential change of just one justice in the U.S. Supreme Court.

The story of *Griswold* begins in 1961, when Estelle, then executive director of the Planned Parenthood League of Connecticut, and Dr. C. Lee Buxton of Yale University's Medical School opened a small birth-control clinic in downtown New Haven, Conn. They intended to challenge the validity of the state's official ban on birth control, and indeed, nine days later, they were arrested for dispensing contraceptives to a married couple. A month later they were convicted and fined $100 each.

When their case finally reached the Supreme Court, seven of nine justices agreed that a zone of privacy safe-guarding birth control inheres in what Justice William O. Douglas called a "penumbra" (a shaded rim between darkness and light) of the Constitution and the Bill of Rights. (Other justices felt it was covered by protections against search and seizure and other specific rights that could logically be extended to cover marriage.) In other words, although the Constitution and the Bill of Rights do not explicitly guarantee privacy rights to individuals, such rights are implicit within the documents.

The landmark ruling in *Griswold v. Connecticut* paved the way for *Eisenstadt v. Baird*, the 1972 Supreme Court decision that extended these same privacy protections—and thus the right to obtain birth control—to unmarried women. It opened the door the following year to the historic ruling in *Roe v. Wade*, which expanded the privacy doctrine to abortion, granting women and their doctors the legal right not just to prevent, but also to terminate, unwanted early pregnancies. Just two years ago, the Court once again drew upon the *Griswold* doctrine of privacy, in the 2003 decision *Lawrence v. Texas*, to protect the right of consensual homosexual relations.

With social conservatives again ascendant across the land—and an intense battle looming over possible Supreme Court vacancies—*Griswold*'s 40th anniversary this year [2005] compels us to remember just how long and hard American progressives have battled to secure reproductive-health rights in this country. It reminds us, as well, how much is at stake today as conservatives challenge our long-protected freedoms under the rubric of trying to prevent abortions, and hurl allegations of "judicial activism" at judges with whose decisions they disagree.

A Comstock Law

The *Griswold* decision overturned. an 1879 Connecticut statute that placed broad criminal sanctions on sexual speech and commerce, including all materials related to sexuality, birth control and abortion. It was the last vestige of the long and infamous legacy of Anthony Comstock, a self-appointed moral arbiter whose evangelical fervor had captured Victorian-era politics and left an enduring web of state and federal statutes intended to root out and prohibit behavior that he, and those who embraced his cause, considered obscene or sinful.

Comstock exploited the inevitable tensions of gender, race and class that beset American society during the fast-paced years of industrialization and urbanization following the Civil War, a turbulent era not dissimilar from our own. He not only helped pass laws, but also had himself authorized as a special agent of the U.S. Postal Service, with the power to undertake searches and make arrests. In his later years, he famously indicted (though failed to convict) birth-control pioneer Margaret Sanger for daring to encourage women to practice family planning. He then framed, arrested and jailed her husband, William, for handling out a pamphlet that provided explicit instructions on various traditional birth-control techniques.

The Growth of a Movement

A year later, following Comstock's death, Margaret Sanger did serve time in jail for handing out diaphragms to immigrant women—in a clinic she opened as a direct challenge to New York's Comstock laws. On appeal, she established the right of doctors in some states to prescribe birth control. Such incidents emboldened Sanger to devote her life to fundamental social change. Over the course of the next 50 years, she built a fledgling coalition of women's-rights advocates, civil libertarians, physicians and social scientists into an enduring family-planning apparatus. Intent on anchoring law and public policy in rational argument and not religious belief, these courageous women and men overturned much of Comstock's handiwork through incremental victories in courts and legislatures. They were not able, however, to supersede local regulations in Catholic-dominated states, such as Connecticut and Massachusetts.

Despite these constraints, the modern family-planning movement continued to grow. During the 1960s, the birth control pill was successfully marketed by a team of scientists and doctors whom Sanger had encouraged and helped fund.

Under President Lyndon Johnson, the federal government incorporated family planning into the nation's domestic anti-poverty programs and began to commit the nation's foreign-policy resources—if only a small fraction—to international population programs. When Sanger was past 80 and confined to a nursing home in Tucson, Ariz., she learned of the Supreme Court decision in *Griswold v. Connecticut* that finally offered universal, constitutional protection for these advances.

What motivated Margaret Sanger and Estelle Griswold was more than a simple desire for freedom in this most private of matters—the decision of whether or not to bear a child. These pioneers of modern feminism also understood that the ability to plan and space one's family is a necessary condition for women to achieve equality in all walks of life. Safe and reliable contraception offers women fundamental control over their bodies and their lives.

So Much at Stake

Roe v. Wade, adopted by a comfortable 7-2 majority of the Court, extended privacy protections to early terminations of unwanted pregnancy. In 1992, however, in deciding the Pennsylvania case *Planned Parenthood v. Casey*, the Court only narrowly (5-4) upheld the core privacy doctrine of *Roe*—and at the same time introduced a new standard that has allowed many states to place greater restrictions on abortion, even in the first trimester. Twenty-four-hour waiting periods and parental-consent laws, for example, have been widely adopted on grounds that they do not constitute what the Court established as "undue burdens," even though for many women they effectively restrict access to abortion procedures.

Considering the close call in *Casey*, the appointment of just one new conservative justice to the Court could threaten *all* constitutional protections for abortion—and perhaps for contraception, as well—thereby reversing history and sending the responsibility for regulating these practices back to politicians in state legislatures. And that's where the Comstock laws were first created so many years ago.

So much is at stake. Before birth control and abortion were legally and readily available, the average woman would become pregnant between 12 and 15 times in her lifetime. Even today in the United States, nearly half of all pregnancies remain unintended, and nearly half of those result in abortion. This is why polls show that the vast majority of Americans reject the extremism of a determined minority and do not want the Supreme Court decisions that protect their private decisions to be overturned. Doctrines of privacy and equality for women are simply not separable: Eroding one imperils the other.

And all this rests on the shoulders of just one new justice.

| "There is not a generalized, abstract right to privacy unhinged from any constitutional text."

The Right to Privacy Identified in *Griswold* Was a Mistake

Rich Lowry

Rich Lowry is editor of National Review *and a commentator for the* Fox News Channel.

In the following viewpoint, although Lowry agrees that there are specific rights to privacy in certain situations identified in the U.S. Constitution, he argues that there is no general right to privacy. He recounts how the right to privacy was first identified in Griswold v. Connecticut, *wherein the Supreme Court used this right to find laws restricting contraception for married persons unconstitutional. Lowry believes that the U.S. Supreme Court's use of the right to privacy in* Griswold *and later cases was misguided, essentially creating a right out of nothing. Lowry comments on how the right to privacy has evolved since* Griswold, *lamenting its use to make decisions that he believes should only be made by legislatures and not by the Supreme Court.*

When the Senate confirmation hearings [in September 2005] for Judge John Roberts begin in a few weeks, his Democratic questioners are sure to obsess on something that doesn't exist: a generalized right to privacy. It was this non-right that was the focus of the successful attack on the [1987] nomination of Judge Robert Bork, when he was impolite enough to note that such a right appears nowhere in the U.S. Constitution. This prompted Democrats to warn that Bork wanted the sex police to patrol America's bedrooms.

The Right to Privacy

The right to privacy is a natural point of attack for Democrats since it is at the root of the Supreme Court's lawlessness that has allowed the justices to anoint themselves as our moral betters and strike down any legislation they find distasteful or retrograde. Without it, liberals might have to fight against laws they oppose—e.g., prohibitions on gay marriage—at the ballot box rather than hope they get struck down by agreeable judges.

In a draft article for Attorney General William French Smith in 1981, Roberts wrote: "All of us may heartily endorse a 'right to privacy.' That does not, however, mean that courts should discern such an abstraction in the Constitution, arbitrarily elevate it over other constitutional rights and powers by attaching the label 'fundamental,' and then resort to it as, in the words of one of Justice [Hugo] Black's dissents, a 'loose, flexible, uncontrolled standard for holding laws unconstitutional.'" Just so.

There are privacy rights in the Constitution. The Fourth Amendment, for example, prohibits unreasonable searches and seizures. The entire constitutional scheme is meant to limit government power and leave people alone most of the time. But there is not a generalized, abstract right to privacy unhinged from any constitutional text.

The Role of *Griswold*

The mischief began 40 years ago in the case *Griswold v. Connecticut* [1965], when the Court struck down a prohibition on contraceptives on the basis of a "right to marital privacy." The bit about "marital" was quickly dropped, and the new discovery became a general right to privacy.

In *Griswold*, the Court suggested the right might be found in the First, Third, Fourth, Fifth and/or Ninth Amendments. In other words, it must be there somewhere, anywhere. But since the right to privacy is nowhere mentioned, the Court had to contend that it resides in "penumbras formed by emanations." In layman's terms, that means in partial shadows formed by emissions, which it doesn't take a constitutional scholar to conclude sounds pretty vaporous.

If Connecticut's contraceptive law was outdated and purposeless, the answer was simple: for voters to overturn it. Both the dissenters in the case, Justices Hugo Black and Potter Stewart noted that they opposed the Connecticut policy, but that didn't make it unconstitutional.

The Evolution of the Right

Roe v. Wade [1973] relied on the same amorphous right to privacy and featured the same tenuous or nonexistent constitutional reasoning. In his decision, Justice Harry Blackmun cited the American Medical Association, the American Public Health Association, the American Bar Association and—but, of course—the "Ephesian, Soranos, often described as the greatest of the ancient gynecologists."

"'Privacy' [has] functioned as a euphemism for immunity from those public-morals laws deemed by the justices to reflect benighted moral views," write scholars Robert P. George and David L. Tubbs. From a right for married couples to obtain contraceptives, it has evolved into a constitutional right of homosexuals to engage in sodomy (in the case of *Lawrence v. Texas* in 2003) and then the right of gays to marry, in a 2003 Massachusetts-supreme-court decision.

The Court has created rights from nothing before. As George and Tubbs point out, from 1890 to 1937, it struck down social-welfare legislation because it supposedly violated a right to "liberty of contract" that had no constitutional basis. It reversed course in 1937 and admitted it had been imposing its own policy preferences. The Supreme Court won't return to its proper, limited role in American governance until it does the same with the mythical "right to privacy."

> "The right to privacy . . . animates the
> entire Constitution, Bill of Rights in-
> cluded."

The Right to Privacy
Identified in *Griswold*
Was Not a Mistake

Jay Bookman

*Jay Bookman is a columnist and the deputy editorial page editor
of the* Atlanta Journal-Constitution, *specializing in foreign relations and environmental and technology-related issues.*

*In the following viewpoint, Bookman argues that the U.S.
Constitution does support the general right to privacy first identified in* Griswold v. Connecticut, *wherein the Supreme Court
ruled that state laws restricting the use of contraception within
marriage violated this privacy right. He disagrees with commentators such as Rich Lowry, who claim that without a right to
privacy explicitly stated in the Constitution, such a right does
not exist. Bookman claims that the history of the adoption of the
Bill of Rights shows that the Founding Fathers meant for a general right to privacy to be implicit. Bookman worries that if this
right to privacy is eliminated, the door will be open to a variety
of government intrusions that will give the majority a frighten-
ing amount of power over the minority.*

Do the American people have a right to privacy?

Absolutely we do. But how long we'll enjoy that right is
very much up in the air.

Jay Bookman, "Privacy Right Unlisted, but Perfectly Clear," *Atlanta Journal-Constitution*,
August 11, 2005, p. A15. Copyright © 2005 by *The Atlanta Journal-Constitution*. Repub-
lished with permission of *The Atlanta Journal-Constitution*, conveyed through Copyright
Clearance Center, Inc.

For now, though, the right to privacy is destined to be debated endlessly when the U.S. Senate takes up President [George W.] Bush's nomination of John Roberts to the Supreme Court [in September 2005].

A Contentious Right

Much of the attention over Roberts' nomination, and much of our nation's obsession with judicial nominations in general, can be traced to the controversial *Roe v. Wade* [1973] decision on abortion. That case was decided on grounds that we do have a constitutional right to privacy, that certain matters are too intimate and personal to allow government to intrude.

In attacking *Roe v. Wade*, the anti-abortion movement argues the right to privacy is a fantasy, a "non-right," as columnist Rich Lowry calls it in the conservative *National Review*. That non-right, Lowry claims, "is at the root of the Supreme Court's lawlessness that has allowed the justices to anoint themselves as our moral betters and strike down any legislation they find distasteful or retrograde."

As Lowry points out, there is no explicit language in the Constitution about privacy, no specific amendment in the Bill of Rights guaranteeing us the right to be left alone. In fact, the legal phrase "right to privacy" dates back only to 1965, when it emerged in a Supreme Court decision in *Griswold v. Connecticut*.

Under Connecticut law, it was a crime to provide married couples with contraceptives, or even to counsel married couples on how to avoid conception. The U.S. Supreme Court overturned that law, sensibly ruling that it violated a married couple's constitutional right to make their own decisions about whether to have children.

Of course, there is no such right in the Constitution, not explicitly anyway. So how did the court make its decision?

The answer lies in the Bill of Rights and American history.

Origin of the Right to Privacy

Many of the strongest advocates of liberty among our Founding Fathers had argued against adopting a Bill of Rights. They feared that listing certain explicit constitutional rights—the right to pray and speak as you wish, for example—might imply that other unlisted natural rights have no standing. In essence, they argued that if we can't list all of our rights as human beings, we shouldn't list any at all.

"This is one of the most plausible arguments I have ever heard urged against the admission of a bill of rights into this system," James Madison acknowledged in introducing his proposed Bill of Rights to Congress in 1789.

To solve that problem, Madison suggested what soon became the Ninth Amendment.

It states, in its entirety:

"The enumeration in the Constitution of certain rights shall not be construed to deny or disparage others retained by the people."

That is a blunt, unequivocal rejection of the anti-abortion stance on the right to privacy. It obliterates the argument that since the right to privacy is not listed explicitly in the Constitution, it must not exist.

We do have a constitutional right to privacy. The right to speak as you wish, to pray as you wish, to be secure in your home against warrantless searches or seizures, are all based on the same underlying right to be left alone by government. The right to privacy, in fact, animates the entire Constitution, Bill of Rights included. The drafters of those documents felt no need to state what in their minds was already so obvious.

The Danger of the Majority

Furthermore, if the Bill of Rights did not include an express ban on laws that tried to tell couples how many children to have, there was a very good reason. Not even King George, tyrannical as he was, would have dared to infringe on something so private.

If the American people eventually lose the right to privacy against an intrusive government, if that protection is eventually removed from us by a more aggressive Supreme Court, a door swings open to a whole variety of government acts.

And as we've seen, most notably in the Terri Schiavo case [the brain-damaged, comatose woman who became the center of a controversial, national right-to-life battle before removal of her feeding tube in 2005], there are politically powerful forces in this country eager to stick government's nose into aspects of our private lives where it has no business being, eager to claim the power of the majority to impose its will.

But in explaining why the Bill of Rights was necessary, Madison warned that the greatest danger to liberty, the most worrisome source of tyranny, "is not found in either the executive or legislative departments of government, but in the body of the people, operating by the majority against the minority." The Bill of Rights, he said, may be "one means to control the majority from those acts to which they might be otherwise inclined."

It has done that job well. So far.

CHAPTER 2

Laws Banning Birth Control for Unmarried Persons Are Unconstitutional

Case Overview

Eisenstadt v. Baird (1972)

In the case of *Eisenstadt v. Baird*, the U.S. Supreme Court determined that the constitutional right to privacy protects the rights of all adults, whether married or unmarried, to use birth control, or contraception. The Court in *Griswold v. Connecticut* (1965) had first recognized the right to privacy, concluding that it protected the right of married persons to use contraception. In *Eisenstadt*, the Court concluded that if the right to privacy allowed married persons access to contraception, it must also allow unmarried persons access to contraception because of the Fourteenth Amendment. The equal protection clause of the Fourteenth Amendment demands that "no state shall ... deny to any person within its jurisdiction the equal protection of the laws."

In 1967 activist William Baird gave a lecture at Boston University on birth control methods and distributed contraceptive devices to those interested. Baird was neither a physician nor a pharmacist. He was arrested and convicted under a Massachusetts law that prevented distribution of contraception by unlicensed individuals and also to unmarried individuals. The Massachusetts Supreme Judicial Court upheld Baird's conviction, but the First Circuit Court of Appeals reversed it. Sheriff Thomas Eisenstadt then appealed the case to the U.S. Supreme Court.

On appeal to the U.S. Supreme Court, the state's justifications for the laws treating unmarried persons differently from married persons were considered and rejected. The Court rejected Massachusetts's claim that all contraceptives require distribution by doctors and pharmacists, noting that most contraceptives were safe and easily self-administered. The Court also rejected the state's argument for restricting contraception to married persons based on morals. The Court concluded that single people, like married persons, have a right to privacy protecting their use of contraception. In this way, the *Eisenstadt* ruling augmented the *Griswold* ruling by determining that the right to make reproductive decisions belonged to individuals and was not conditional on marriage.

William J. Brennan's explanation of the right to privacy in *Eisenstadt* has been frequently quoted in subsequent Supreme Court opinions dealing with reproductive privacy: "If the right of privacy means anything, it is the right of the individual, married or single, to be free from unwarranted governmental intrusion into matters so fundamentally affecting a person as the decision whether to bear or beget a child." This strong assertion of the right to reproductive autonomy went on to underpin some of the Court's later landmark decisions, such as *Roe v. Wade*.

> *"It is the right of an individual, married or single, to be free from unwarranted governmental intrusion into matters so fundamentally affecting a person as the decision whether to bear or beget a child."*

Majority Opinion: The Right to Privacy in Contraception Extends to Unmarried Individuals

William J. Brennan Jr.

William J. Brennan Jr. was a justice of the U.S. Supreme Court from 1956 to 1990. He was an outspoken liberal and is considered to be one of the more influential justices to have sat on the Court.

The following is the majority opinion in the 1972 case of Eisenstadt v. Baird, *wherein the Supreme Court determined that the constitutional right to privacy protects the rights of all adults, whether married or unmarried, to use contraception. William Baird was convicted under a Massachusetts law preventing distribution of contraception. After the lower court upheld Baird's conviction, the court of appeals discharged it. On appeal to the U.S. Supreme Court, the state's justifications for the laws treating unmarried persons differently from married persons were considered and rejected as a violation of the equal protection clause of the Fourteenth Amendment. The Court concluded that single people, like married people, have a right to privacy protecting their use of contraception.*

William J. Brennan Jr., majority opinion, *Eisenstadt v. Baird*, U.S. Supreme Court, March 22, 1972.

Appellee William Baird was convicted at a bench trial in the Massachusetts Superior Court under Massachusetts General Laws Ann., c. 272, § 21, first, for exhibiting contraceptive articles in the course of delivering a lecture on contraception to a group of students at Boston University and, second, for giving a young woman a package of Emko vaginal foam at the close of his address. The Massachusetts Supreme Judicial Court unanimously set aside the conviction for exhibiting contraceptives on the ground that it violated Baird's First Amendment rights, but, by a four-to-three vote, sustained the conviction for giving away the foam. Baird subsequently filed a petition for a federal writ of habeas corpus, which the District Court dismissed. On appeal, however, the Court of Appeals for the First Circuit vacated the dismissal and remanded the action with directions to grant the writ discharging Baird. This appeal by the Sheriff of Suffolk County, Massachusetts, followed, and we noted probable jurisdiction. We affirm.

The Massachusetts Law

Massachusetts General Laws Ann., c. 272, § 21, under which Baird was convicted, provides a maximum five-year term of imprisonment for "whoever . . . gives away . . . any drug, medicine, instrument or article whatever for the prevention of conception," except as authorized in § 21A. Under § 21A, "[a] registered physician may administer to or prescribe for any married person drugs or articles intended for the prevention of pregnancy or conception. [And a] registered pharmacist actually engaged in the business of pharmacy may furnish such drugs or articles to any married person presenting a prescription from a registered physician." As interpreted by the State Supreme Judicial Court, these provisions make it a felony for anyone, other than a registered physician or pharmacist acting in accordance with the terms of § 21A, to dispense any article with the intention that it be used for the prevention of conception. The statutory scheme distinguishes among three distinct classes of distributees—*first*, married persons may obtain contraceptives to prevent pregnancy, but only from doctors or druggists on prescription; *second*, single persons may not obtain contraceptives from anyone to prevent pregnancy; and, *third*, married or single persons may obtain contraceptives from anyone to prevent not pregnancy, but the spread of disease. This construction of state law is, of course, binding on us.

The legislative purposes that the statute is meant to serve are not altogether clear. In *Commonwealth v. Baird* [1969], the Supreme Judicial Court noted only the State's interest in protecting the health of its citizens: "[T]he prohibition in § 21," the court declared, "is directly related to" the State's goal of "preventing the distribution of articles designed to prevent conception which may have undesirable, if not dangerous, physical consequences." In a subsequent decision, *Sturgis v. Attorney General* (1970), the court, however, found "a second and more compelling ground for upholding the statute"—namely, to protect morals through "regulating the private sexual lives of single persons." The Court of Appeals, for reasons that will appear, did not consider the promotion of health or the protection of morals through the deterrence of fornication to be the legislative aim. Instead, the court concluded that the statutory goal was to limit contraception in and of itself—a purpose that the court held conflicted "with fundamental human rights" under *Griswold v. Connecticut* (1965), where this Court struck down Connecticut's prohibition against the use of contraceptives as an unconstitutional infringement of the right of marital privacy.

We agree that the goals of deterring premarital sex and regulating the distribution of potentially harmful articles cannot reasonably be regarded as legislative aims of §§ 21 and 21A. And we hold that the statute, viewed as a prohibition on contraception *per se*, violates the rights of single persons under the Equal Protection Clause of the Fourteenth Amendment. . . .

Different Treatment

The basic principles governing application of the Equal Protection Clause of the Fourteenth Amendment are familiar. As the chief justice [Warren E. Burger] only recently explained in *Reed v. Reed* (1971):

> "In applying that clause, this Court has consistently recognized that the Fourteenth Amendment does not deny to States the power to treat different classes of persons in different ways. The Equal Protection Clause of that amendment does, however, deny to States the power to legislate that different treatment be accorded to persons placed by a statute into different classes on the basis of criteria wholly unrelated to the objective of that statute. A classification 'must be reasonable, not arbitrary, and must rest upon some ground of difference having a fair and substantial relation to the object of the legislation, so that all persons similarly circumstanced shall be treated alike.'"

The question for our determination in this case is whether there is some ground of difference that rationally explains the different treatment accorded married and unmarried persons under Massachusetts General Laws Ann., c. 272, §§ 21 and 21A. For the reasons that follow, we conclude that no such ground exists. *First.* Section 21 stems from Mass.Stat. 1879, c. 159, § 1, which prohibited, without exception, distribution of articles intended to be used as contraceptives. In *Commonwealth v. Allison* (1917), the Massachusetts Supreme Judicial Court explained that the law's "plain purpose is to protect purity, to preserve chastity, to encourage continence and self-restraint, to defend the sanctity of the home, and thus to engender in the State and nation a virile and virtuous race of men and women." Although the State clearly abandoned that purpose with the enactment of § 21A, at least insofar as the illicit sexual activities of married persons are concerned, the court reiterated in *Sturgis v. Attorney General* that the object of the legislation is to discourage premarital sexual intercourse. Conceding that the State could, consistently with the Equal Protection Clause, regard the problems of extramarital and premarital sexual relations as "[e]vils ... of different dimensions and proportions, requiring different remedies," *Williamson v. Lee Optical Co.* (1955), we cannot agree that the deterrence of premarital sex may reasonably be regarded as the purpose of the Massachusetts law.

It would be plainly unreasonable to assume that Massachusetts has prescribed pregnancy and the birth of an unwanted child as punishment for fornication, which is a misdemeanor under Massachusetts General Laws Ann., c. 272, § 18. Aside from the scheme of values that assumption would attribute to the State, it is abundantly clear that the effect of the ban on distribution of contraceptives to unmarried persons has, at best, a marginal relation to the proffered objective. What Mr. Justice [Arthur] Goldberg said in *Griswold v. Connecticut* concerning the effect of Connecticut's prohibition on the use of contraceptives in discouraging extramarital sexual relations, is equally applicable here. "The rationality of this justification is dubious, particularly in light of the admitted widespread availability to all persons in the State of Connecticut, unmarried as well as married, of birth control devices for the prevention of disease, as distinguished from the prevention of conception." Like Connecticut's laws, §§ 21 and 21A do not at all regulate the distribution of contraceptives when they are to be used to prevent, not pregnancy, but the spread of disease. Nor, in making contraceptives available to married persons without regard to their intended use, does Massachusetts attempt to deter married persons from engaging in illicit sexual relations with unmarried persons. Even on the assumption that the fear of pregnancy operates as a deterrent to fornication, the Massachusetts statute is thus so riddled with exceptions that deterrence of premarital sex cannot reasonably be regarded as its aim.

Moreover, §§ 21 and 21A, on their face, have a dubious relation to the State's criminal prohibition on fornication. As the Court of Appeals explained, "Fornication is a misdemeanor [in Massachusetts], entailing a thirty dollar fine, or three months in jail. Violation of the present statute is a felony, punishable by five years in prison. We find it hard to believe that the legislature adopted a statute carrying a five-year penalty for its possible, obviously by no means fully effective, deterrence of the commission of a ninety-day misdemeanor." Even conceding the legislature a full measure of discretion in fashioning means to prevent fornication, and recognizing that the State may seek to deter prohibited conduct by punishing more severely those who facilitate than those who actually engage in its commission, we, like the Court of Appeals, cannot believe that, in this instance, Massachusetts has chosen to expose the aider and abetter who simply gives away a contraceptive to *20* times the 90-day sentence of the offender himself. The very terms of the State's criminal statutes, coupled with the *de minimis* [minimal] effect of §§ 21 and 21A in deterring fornication, thus compel the conclusion that such deterrence cannot reasonably be taken as the purpose of the ban on distribution of contraceptives to unmarried persons.

The Rationale of Health

Second. Section 21A was added to the Massachusetts General Laws by Stat. 1966, c. 265, § 1. The Supreme Judicial Court, in *Commonwealth v. Baird*, held that the purpose of the amendment was to serve the health needs of the community by regulating the distribution of potentially harmful articles. It is plain that Massachusetts had no such purpose in mind before the enactment of § 21A. As the Court of Appeals remarked, "Consistent with the fact that the statute was contained in a chapter dealing with 'Crimes Against Chastity, Morality, Decency and Good Order,' it was cast only in terms of morals. A physician was forbidden to prescribe contraceptives even when needed for the protection of health." Nor did the Court of Appeals "believe that the legislature [in enacting § 21A] suddenly reversed its field and developed an interest in health. Rather, it merely made what it thought to be the precise accommodation necessary to escape the *Griswold* ruling."

Again, we must agree with the Court of Appeals. If health were the rationale of § 21A, the statute would be both discriminatory and overbroad. Dissenting in *Commonwealth v. Baird*, Justices [Arthur Easterbrook] Whittemore and [R. Ammi] Cutter stated that they saw "in § 21 and § 21A, read together, no public health purpose. If there is need to have a physician prescribe (and a pharmacist dispense) contraceptives, that need is as great for unmarried persons as for married persons." The Court of Appeals added: "If the prohibition [on distribution to unmarried persons] . . . is to be taken to mean that the same physician who can prescribe for married patients does not have sufficient skill to protect the health of patients who lack a marriage certificate, or who may be currently divorced, it is illogical to the point of irrationality." Furthermore, we must join the Court of Appeals in noting that not all contraceptives are potentially dangerous. As a result, if the Massachusetts statute were a health measure, it would not only invidiously discriminate against the unmarried, but also be overbroad with respect to the married, a fact that the Supreme Judicial Court itself seems to have conceded in *Sturgis v. Attorney General*, where it noted that "it may well be that certain contraceptive medication and devices constitute no hazard to health, in which event it could be argued that the statute swept too broadly in its prohibition." "In this posture," as the Court of Appeals concluded, "it is impossible to think of the statute as intended as a health measure for the unmarried, and it is almost as difficult to think of it as so intended even as to the married."

But if further proof that the Massachusetts statute is not a health measure is necessary, the argument of Justice [Jacob J.]

Spiegel, who also dissented in *Commonwealth v. Baird*, is conclusive: "It is, at best, a strained conception to say that the Legislature intended to prevent the distribution of articles 'which may have undesirable, if not dangerous, physical consequences.' If that was the Legislature's goal, § 21 is not required" in view of the federal and state laws *already* regulating the distribution of harmful drugs. We conclude, accordingly, that, despite the statute's superficial earmarks as a health measure, health, on the face of the statute, may no more reasonably be regarded as its purpose than the deterrence of premarital sexual relations.

The Relevance of *Griswold*

Third. If the Massachusetts statute cannot be upheld as a deterrent to fornication or as a health measure, may it, nevertheless, be sustained simply as a prohibition on contraception? The Court of Appeals analysis "led inevitably to the conclusion that, so far as morals are concerned, it is contraceptives *per se* that are considered immoral—to the extent that *Griswold* will permit such a declaration." The Court of Appeals went on to hold:

> "To say that contraceptives are immoral as such, and are to be forbidden to unmarried persons who will nevertheless persist in having intercourse, means that such persons must risk for themselves an unwanted pregnancy, for the child, illegitimacy, and, for society, a possible obligation of support. Such a view of morality is not only the very mirror image of sensible legislation; we consider that it conflicts with fundamental human rights. In the absence of demonstrated harm, we hold it is beyond the competency of the state."

We need not, and do not, however, decide that important question in this case, because, whatever the rights of the individual to access to contraceptives may be, the rights must be the same for the unmarried and the married alike.

If, under *Griswold*, the distribution of contraceptives to married persons cannot be prohibited, a ban on distribution to unmarried persons would be equally impermissible. It is true that, in *Griswold*, the right of privacy in question inhered in the marital relationship. Yet the marital couple is not an independent entity, with a mind and heart of its own, but an association of two individuals, each with a separate intellectual and emotional makeup. If the right of privacy means anything, it is the right of the individual, married or single, to be free from unwarranted governmental intrusion into matters so fundamentally affecting a person as the decision whether to bear or beget a child.

On the other hand, if *Griswold* is no bar to a prohibition on the distribution of contraceptives, the State could not, consistently with the Equal Protection Clause, outlaw distribution to unmarried, but not to married, persons. In each case, the evil, as perceived by the State, would be identical, and the underinclusion would be invidious. Mr. Justice [Robert H.] Jackson, concurring in *Railway Express Agency v. New York* (1949), made the point:

> "The framers of the Constitution knew, and we should not forget today, that there is no more effective practical guaranty against arbitrary and unreasonable government than to require that the principles of law which officials would impose upon a minority must be imposed generally. Conversely, nothing opens the door to arbitrary action so effectively as to allow those officials to pick and choose only a few to whom they will apply legislation, and thus to escape the political retribution that might be visited upon them if larger numbers were affected. Courts can take no better measure to assure that laws will be just than to require that laws be equal in operation."

Although Mr. Justice Jackson's comments had reference to administrative regulations, the principle he affirmed has equal application to the legislation here. We hold that, by providing dissimilar treatment for married and unmarried persons who are similarly situated, Massachusetts General Laws Ann., c. 272, §§ 21 and 21A, violate the Equal Protection Clause.

"I see nothing in . . . the Constitution that even vaguely suggests that . . . contraceptives must be available in the open market."

Dissenting Opinion: The Constitution Allows State Regulation of Contraception

Warren E. Burger

Warren E. Burger was chief justice of the United States from 1969 to 1986. Nominated to the Court by President Richard M. Nixon, Burger was considered a conservative and a strict constructionist, committed to making judicial decisions based only on the text of law.

The following is Burger's dissenting opinion in the 1972 case of Eisenstadt v. Baird. *Burger argues that there is no constitutional basis for the Court to question a state's purpose for a law restricting access to contraception, because states have the power to regulate products in the area of health. He concludes that the Court overstepped its authority in determining that a constitutional right to privacy in reproduction disallowed Massachusetts's regulation of contraception.*

The judgment of the Supreme Judicial Court of Massachusetts in sustaining appellee's conviction for dispensing medicinal material without a license seems eminently correct to me, and I would not disturb it. It is undisputed that appellee is not a physician or pharmacist, and was prohibited under

Warren E. Burger, dissenting opinion, *Eisenstadt v. Baird*, U.S. Supreme Court, March 22, 1972.

Massachusetts law from dispensing contraceptives to anyone, regardless of marital status. To my mind, the validity of this restriction on dispensing medicinal substances is the only issue before the Court, and appellee has no standing to challenge that part of the statute restricting the persons to whom contraceptives are available. There is no need to labor this point, however, for everyone seems to agree that, if Massachusetts has validly required, as a health measure, that all contraceptives be dispensed by a physician or pursuant to a physician's prescription, then the statutory distinction based on marital status has no bearing on this case.

The Majority and Concurring Opinions

The opinion of the Court today brushes aside appellee's status as an unlicensed layman by concluding that the Massachusetts Legislature was not really concerned with the protection of health when it passed this statute. Mr. Justice [Byron] White acknowledges [in his concurrence] the statutory concern with the protection of health, but finds the restriction on distributors overly broad because the State has failed to adduce facts showing the health hazards of the particular substance dispensed by appellee as distinguished from other contraceptives. Mr. Justice [William O.] Douglas' concurring opinion does not directly challenge the power of Massachusetts to prohibit laymen from dispensing contraceptives, but considers that appellee, rather than dispensing the substance, was resorting to a "time-honored teaching technique" by utilizing a "visual aid" as an adjunct to his protected speech. I am puzzled by this third characterization of the case. If the suggestion is that appellee was merely displaying the contraceptive material without relinquishing his ownership of it, then the argument must be that the prosecution failed to prove that appellee had "given away" the contraceptive material. But appellee does not challenge the sufficiency of the evidence, and himself summarizes the record as showing that, "at the close of his lecture, he invited members of the audience ... to come and help themselves." On the other hand, if the concurring opinion means that the First Amendment protects the distribution of all articles "not dangerous *per se*" when the distribution is coupled with some form of speech, then I must confess that I have misread certain cases in the area.

My disagreement with the opinion of the Court and that of Mr. Justice White goes far beyond mere puzzlement, however, for these opinions seriously invade the constitutional prerogatives of the States, and regrettably hark back to the heyday of substantive due process.

Rejection of a State Purpose

In affirming appellee's conviction, the highest tribunal in Massachusetts held that the statutory requirement that contraceptives be dispensed only through medical channels served the legitimate interest of the State in protecting the health of its citizens. The Court today blithely hurdles this authoritative state pronouncement and concludes that the statute has no such purpose. Three basic arguments are advanced: first, since the distribution of contraceptives was prohibited as a moral matter in Massachusetts prior to 1966, it is impossible to believe that the legislature was concerned with health when it lifted the complete ban, but insisted on medical supervision. I fail to see why the historical predominance of an unacceptable legislative purpose makes incredible the emergence of a new and valid one. The second argument, finding its origin in a dissenting opinion in the Supreme Judicial Court of Massachusetts, rejects a health purpose because, "[i]f there is need to have a physician prescribe ... contraceptives, that need is as great for unmarried persons as for married persons." This argument confuses the validity of the restriction on distributors with the validity of the further restriction on distributees, a part of the statute not properly before the Court. Assuming the legislature too broadly restricted the class of persons who could obtain contraceptives, it hardly follows that it saw no need to protect the health of all persons to whom they are made available. Third, the Court sees no health purpose underlying the restriction on distributors, because other state and federal laws regulate the distribution of harmful drugs. I know of no rule that all enactments relating to a particular purpose must be neatly consolidated in one package in the statute books, for, if so, the United States Code will not pass muster. I am unable to draw any inference as to legislative purpose from the fact that the restriction on dispensing contraceptives was not codified with other statutory provisions regulating the distribution of medicinal substances. And the existence of nonconflicting, nonpreemptive federal laws is simply without significance in judging the validity or purpose of a state law on the same subject matter.

It is possible, of course, that some members of the Massachusetts Legislature desired contraceptives to be dispensed only through medical channels in order to minimize their use, rather than to protect the health of their users, but I do not think it is the proper function of this Court to dismiss, as dubious, a state court's explication of a state statute absent overwhelming and irrefutable reasons for doing so.

The State's Power to Regulate

Mr. Justice White, while acknowledging a valid legislative purpose of protecting health, concludes that the State lacks power to regulate the distribution of the contraceptive involved in this case as a means of protecting health. The opinion grants that appellee's conviction would be valid if he had given away a potentially harmful substance, but rejects the State's placing this particular contraceptive in that category. So far as I am aware, this Court has never before challenged the police power of a State to protect the public from the risks of possibly spurious and deleterious substances sold within its borders. Moreover, a statutory classification is not invalid "simply because some innocent articles or transactions may be found within the proscribed class. The inquiry must be whether, considering the end in view, the statute passes the bounds of reason and assumes the character of a merely arbitrary fiat."

But since the Massachusetts statute seeks to protect health by regulating contraceptives, the opinion invokes *Griswold v. Connecticut* (1965), and puts the statutory classification to an unprecedented test: either the record must contain evidence supporting the classification or the health hazards of the particular contraceptive must be judicially noticeable. This is indeed a novel constitutional doctrine, and, not surprisingly, no authority is cited for it.

Since the potential harmfulness of this particular medicinal substance has never been placed in issue in the state or federal courts, the State can hardly be faulted for its failure to build a record on this point. And it totally mystifies me why, in the absence of some evidence in the record, the factual underpinnings of the statutory classification must be "incontrovertible," or a matter of "common knowledge."

The actual hazards of introducing a particular foreign substance into the human body are frequently controverted, and I cannot believe that unanimity of expert opinion is a prerequisite to a State's exercise of its police power, no matter what the subject matter of the regulation. Even assuming no present dispute among medical authorities, we cannot ignore that it has become commonplace for a drug or food additive to be universally regarded as harmless on one day and to be condemned as perilous on the next. It is inappropriate for this Court to overrule a legislative classification by relying on the present consensus among leading authorities. The commands of the Constitution cannot fluctuate with the shifting tides of scientific opinion.

Even if it were conclusively established once and for all that the product dispensed by appellee is not actually or potentially dangerous in the somatic sense, I would still be unable to agree that the restriction on dispensing it falls outside the State's power to regulate in the area of health. The choice of a means of birth control, although a highly personal matter, is also a health matter in a very real sense, and I see nothing arbitrary in a requirement of medical supervision. It is generally acknowledged that contraceptives vary in degree of effectiveness and potential harmfulness. There may be compelling health reasons for certain women to choose the most effective means of birth control available, no matter how harmless the less effective alternatives. Others might be advised not to use a highly effective means of contraception because of their peculiar susceptibility to an adverse side effect. Moreover, there may be information known to the medical profession that a particular brand of contraceptive is to be preferred or avoided, or that it has not been adequately tested. Nonetheless, the concurring opinion would hold, as a constitutional matter, that a State must allow someone without medical training the same power to distribute this medicinal substance as is enjoyed by a physician.

No Constitutional Support

It is revealing, I think, that those portions of the majority and concurring opinions rejecting the statutory limitation on distributors rely on no particular provision of the Constitution. I see nothing in the Fourteenth Amendment or any other part of the Constitution that even vaguely suggests that these medicinal forms of contraceptives must be available in the open market. I do not challenge *Griswold v. Connecticut*, despite its tenuous moorings to the text of the Constitution, but I cannot view it as controlling authority for this case. The Court was there confronted with a statute flatly prohibiting the use of contraceptives, not one regulating their distribution. I simply cannot believe that the limitation on the class of lawful distributors has significantly impaired the right to use contraceptives in Massachusetts. By relying on *Griswold* in the present context, the Court has passed beyond the penumbras of the specific guarantees into the uncircumscribed area of personal predilections.

The need for dissemination of information on birth control is not impinged in the slightest by limiting the distribution of medicinal substances to medical and pharmaceutical channels, as Massachusetts has done by statute. The appellee has succeeded, it seems, in cloaking his activities in some new permutation of the First Amendment, although his conviction rests, in fact and law, on dispensing a medicinal substance without a license. I am constrained to suggest that, if the Constitution can be strained to invalidate the Massachusetts statute underlying appellee's conviction, we could quite as well employ it for the protection of a "curbstone quack," reminiscent of the "medicine man" of times past, who attracted a crowd of the curious with a soapbox lecture and then plied them with "free samples" of some unproved remedy. Massachusetts presumably outlawed such activities long ago, but today's holding seems to invite their return.

> "The [Eisenstadt] decision is among the
> most influential in the United States
> during the entire century by any man-
> ner or means of measurement."

Eisenstadt Is One of the Most Influential Supreme Court Cases

Roy Lucas

*Roy Lucas was a lawyer who first articulated how the Supreme
Court's 1965* Griswold v. Connecticut *decision could be expanded into a constitutional protection for a woman's right to
an abortion.*

*In the following viewpoint, Lucas contends that the puritani-
cal Massachusetts law preventing distribution of contraception
ended up having a huge impact on history by the way it was
found unconstitutional in* Eisenstadt v. Baird, *wherein the Supreme Court extended to unmarried people the right to privacy
in the use of contraceptives. Lucas notes that the timing of the
case was critically important and suggests that had it been later
the impact of the case may not have been as great. The specific
wording of the case linking the right to privacy with human reproduction, Lucas contends, provided the foundation for a
woman's right to abortion and affected many other cases.*

From the shadowy, puritanical Victorian days of 1879, until
March 22, 1972, the Commonwealth of Massachusetts pe-
riodically enforced an archaic law that initially defined its
sweeping crime as follows:

Roy Lucas Jr., "New Historical Insights on the Curious Case of *Baird v. Eisenstadt*,"
Roger Williams University Law Review, vol. 9, 2003, pp. 9–12, 33–35, 41–44, 48. Copyright © 2003 Roger Williams University Law Review. Reproduced by permission.

Whoever sells, lends, gives away, exhibits, or offers to sell, lend or give away ... any drug, medicine, instrument or article whatever for the prevention of conception ... or advertises same, or writes, prints, or causes to be written or printed a card, circular, book, pamphlet, advertisement or notice of any kind stating when, where, how, of whom or by what means such article can be purchased or obtained, or manufactures or makes any such article shall be punished by imprisonment in the state prison for not more than five years. . . .

Thus, it was criminal in the Commonwealth to sell, give away, loan, or show contraceptives such as condoms, IUDs [intrauterine devices], birth control pills, and perhaps even rhythm charts. Any transmission of information or means of contraception could come under the prohibition of the law. A user could be a felon as well, or an accessory, or perhaps a conspirator, depending upon the creativity of the prosecutor.

Death of the Massachusetts Law

Any such transmission of contraceptive means or information was initially a crime, whether done by a physician, druggist, or professional teacher-lecturer. The same was true regardless of whether the recipient was married, and irrespective of health or even life concerns which necessitated such use. The 1879 Massachusetts birth control ban, like that of the same year in Connecticut, was total, and has a place of shame in legal history not unlike a scarlet letter [in Nathaniel Hawthorne's 1850 novel *The Scarlet Letter*, the scarlet letter A was worn by persons convicted of adultery].

Law students since the 1940s have studied the path of the Massachusetts mini-Comstock law [named after moralistic U.S. postal inspector Anthony Comstock] from its inception in 1879, the failed challenges of 1938, the successful "right of privacy" case of *Griswold v. Connecticut* in 1965, Massachusetts amendments after *Griswold*, and *Eisenstadt v. Baird* in 1972. The *Abortion Cases of 1973* [*Roe v. Wade* (1973) and *Doe v.*

Bolton (1973)] followed, and relied in significant part upon *Baird* dictum cleverly inserted into the opinion by Justice [William J.] Brennan [Jr.]

Today we can enrich these important historical studies with newly available manuscript papers from the Library of Congress and the National Archives. These papers reveal the United States Supreme Court's previously secret processes of deciding cases defining American constitutional rights. They open up some of the reality behind the stately printed "opinions of the Court," which often are clerk-written, after-the-fact rationalizations, drafted to reinforce the conclusions of our nine highest, secluded, and secretive, black-robe-clad lawyer-judges. . . .

The Court of Appeals Decision

The United States Court of Appeals for the First Circuit heard *Baird v. Eisenstadt* on June 4, 1970 and efficiently decided the case in a four-page opinion released July 6, 1970. The rocket pace from the Supreme Court refusal-to-hear on January 12, 1970 to a full court of appeals decision July 6, 1970 is nothing short of amazing.

Initially, Judge [Bailey] Aldrich rejected out of hand the First Amendment arguments of Baird for "symbolic speech" because acts beyond speech were involved. That analysis was too abbreviated and dismissively conclusory, but the court moved on to rule in Baird's favor.

Aldrich next identified the reasons Massachusetts proffered for the law against giving away contraceptives: "health and morals." The Commonwealth asserted that contraceptives had to be carefully controlled and access limited because of health issues. Further, Massachusetts insisted that it could criminalize transfers of contraceptives altogether to unmarried persons, and that it had the power "to enact statutes regulating the private sexual lives of single persons." The court of appeals found the Commonwealth position "arbitrary and discriminatory" because of "the statute's total exclusion of the unmarried, and because of its palpable overbreadth with respect to the married."

Additionally, the court held specifically that Baird had standing to sue although he was neither a physician nor a pharmacist. Standing followed from the mere circumstance of Baird being criminally prosecuted. The Massachusetts high court itself had recognized standing by suggesting that Baird might instead have brought a declaratory judgment proceeding.

The Commonwealth of Massachusetts promptly appealed the court of appeals' judgment to the Supreme Court. It timely filed its papers as No. 70-17, *Eisenstadt v. Baird*. In sequence, this was just before *Roe v. Wade*, which became No. 70-18, which I had personally filed in the Supreme Court, probably the same day. If *Baird v. Eisenstadt* had been appealed later in the day, or the following day, after *Roe*, it might have been held over for the decisions in the earlier relevant privacy cases, and may not have been argued at all! Instead, by synchronism, *Baird* became a very forceful supporting precedent for *Roe*, *Doe*, and a host of privacy/Equal Protection cases in the decades since. . . .

The Court's Conference Discussion

The [William O.] Douglas, [Thurgood] Marshall, Brennan manuscript papers in the Library of Congress archives tell us what next occurred with *Eisenstadt v. Baird*. The Conference discussion on the case followed on the morning of Friday, November 19, 1971. Chief Justice [Warren E.] Burger opened the *Baird* case discussion indicating his intention to reverse the first circuit and uphold the Massachusetts statute. He summarized his view stating: "this is like cigarettes—a vendor's license is needed." As we shall see, there is no evidence anywhere that Burger had studied the briefs, the record, or any of the lower court opinions. The other Justices simply ignored him in such situations.

Next, the most senior Justice, William O. Douglas, voted for Baird. He found the case to be a straightforward First Amendment matter and Baird's handing out of a can of Emko foam to view was a legitimate part and extension of the educational lecture. Potter Stewart found the statute to be "completely irrational." He supported Justice Brennan (who shortly would be writing the plurality opinion for the Court) and his view that "this is in the penumbra of *Griswold*." Justice [Byron] White initially stated that he was inclined to rule against Baird and reverse, because Baird was not a doctor as the statute required. As to the belated argument by Senator [Joseph] Tydings that federal law might preempt the Massachusetts restrictions, White thought there "might be something to [it]." White eventually wrote a concurring opinion favoring Baird, joined by Justice Harry A. Blackmun who soon was to be writing the opinions in the *Abortion Cases of 1973*.

The unwillingness of Blackmun to support Brennan on privacy at this point, and even later, is enigmatic. Blackmun's physician-oriented focus may have been the cause, or the fact that Brennan and Douglas represented the old Earl Warren Court. Nonetheless, the Blackmun vote for Baird in concurrence with Justice White was an important one, and a deliberate break with Chief Justice Burger.

The Conference discussion made it clear that by November 19, 1971 Baird had prevailed, at least 5-2, but he would not know it until publication of the decision four months later on March 22, 1972. A memorandum in the Douglas archives dated November 23, 1971, indicates that Justice Brennan had initially agreed to prepare a per curiam [i.e., anonymous] opinion, because the views of the Justices had been so diverse. The reality is more complex. Chief Justice Burger, on November 23, stated in a letter to both Douglas and Brennan, "My vote is a questionable reverse with a note 'could affirm—depends on how written.'"

Justice Brennan wasted no time. He was already far ahead of the pack. Brennan was ever the chess grandmaster.

The *Baird* Opinion

No brief per curiam draft opinion emerged from the Brennan chambers. Instead, on December 13, 1971, the date of the *Roe/ Doe* oral argument, Justice Brennan circulated a printed sixteen-page draft of a full opinion on the *Baird* merits. This contained his soon-to-be-famous "bear or beget" language that linked contraception and abortion as part of the overall phenomenon of human reproduction. The ever-quoted sentence from *Baird* is: "If the right of privacy means anything, it is the right of the *individual*, married or single, to be free from unwarranted governmental intrusion into matters so fundamentally affecting a person as the decision whether to bear or beget a child."

This phrase appeared near the end of the *Baird* draft opinions from December 13, 1971. No Justice objected to the expression, and all understood the content and purpose. The phrase has since been quoted literally hundreds of times since 1972 in federal and state court decisions and scholarly articles from one end of the United States to the other, and not infrequently by the Planned Parenthood critics of Baird who had failed in the same mission for over 90 years before Baird came along.

The timing and content were a work of superior intellect and strategy and helped rescue the *Roe/Doe* cases that had been argued in such painfully mediocre fashion by the Texas and Georgia lawyers that very morning. The entire Court now had before it a high-quality privacy and Equal Protection opinion to study before any vote at all on *Roe/Doe*. . . .

Baird's Continuing Impact

Some Supreme Court decisions affect only the parties to the lawsuit, and thereafter seem to disappear forever. Others, such as *Roe v. Wade*, are cited hundreds of times. *Eisenstadt v. Baird* has been cited many hundreds of times. A basic www.Find Law.com search shows *Baird* mentioned in over 52 subsequent Supreme Court cases from 1972 through December 2002. According to Shepard's citator, each and every one of the eleven U.S. Court of Appeals Circuits, as well as the Federal Circuit, has cited *Eisenstadt v. Baird* as authority. Shepard's further reveals that *Baird* has been cited by the highest courts of all 50 States, the District of Columbia, and Puerto Rico, with the last [as of 2003] being Mississippi in the year 2000. Better late than never. Add to that the three columns of law journal articles Shepard's has on *Baird*, and one must acknowledge that the decision is among the most influential in the United States during the entire century by any manner or means of measurement.

| "Nowhere are women given especial fo-
cus in the right to privacy; men retain
the right to procreate or not to procreate."

The Right to Procreate or Not
Should Also Apply to Men

Ethan J. Leib

*Ethan J. Leib is associate professor of law at the University of
California–San Francisco Hastings College of the Law. He is an
affiliated faculty member at the Kadish Center for Morality,
Law, and Public Affairs at the University of California–Berkeley.*

*In the following viewpoint, Leib contends that men's repro-
ductive autonomy needs to be legally recognized. Leib argues for
a nongendered account of procreative choice, relying on text
from the majority opinion in* Eisenstadt v. Baird *for support. In
the* Eisenstadt *case, the Court determined that the right to privacy protected both married and unmarried adults from laws
that restrict contraceptive use. Leib notes that within the opinion, the right to privacy in reproduction is given to both men
and women. Leib laments the move away from this nongendered
right in recent cases and concludes that a man's right to choose
abortion needs to be given weight within the legal system.*

In *Planned Parenthood v. Danforth* (1976), the Supreme
Court made clear that a state could not require a father's
consent before allowing a woman to procure an abortion. And
Planned Parenthood of Southeastern Pennsylvania v. Casey

(1992) struck down as unconstitutional a spousal notification provision, which required a married woman to sign a statement that she had notified her spouse before undergoing an abortion.

Men's Rights to Procreational Autonomy

Does this mean a man has no cognizable interest in the fate of his potential child? Should men be forced to have children against their will? What if they affirmatively want a fetus aborted? Don't they have rights to procreational autonomy too?

Adding insult to injury, men can get slapped with paternity suits (and jailed for failure to pay) even if they wore a condom and never consented to fatherhood. Although one might think that a man implicitly consents to letting his lover choose what happens with his sperm by engaging in consensual sexual relations, basic fairness demands there must be limitations to this logic, particularly given that women can engage in consensual sex without being required to complete any resulting pregnancy.

Might men have a limited right to choose an "abortion" of parental rights and duties in some form? Might they even have a greater right to participate in the abortion decision than *Danforth* and *Casey* suggest? If we are serious about the right to choose, it might be more equitable to be more egalitarian about it.

A Relevant 2005 Case

A February [2005] appeals court decision from Illinois started considering these issues. According to Dr. Richard Phillips, Dr. Sharon Irons performed (consensual) oral sex upon him, but then, unbeknownst to him, used his sperm to conceive a child. Reportedly, soon after she gave birth, Irons slapped Phillips with a paternity suit, in which he was required to pay $800 a month in child support. Thereafter, Phillips sued Irons, inter alia [among other things], for intentional infliction of emotional distress and theft in Cook County Circuit Court; that court dismissed his claims.

The appeals court, however, allowed his case to go forward, saying that he may sue for emotional distress but not theft. The higher court found that Irons could not have stolen the sperm because when Phillips "delivered his sperm, it was a gift. . . . There was no agreement that the original deposit would be returned upon request." Nevertheless, it found that Phillips had a cognizable interest in not becoming a father against his will and gave the suit a green light.

Although it didn't directly raise the issue, the [2005] Illinois case puts in salient relief an understudied area of the abortion debate: what role men should have in the decision to prevent their genetic material from making its way into the world.

A Woman's Right to Choose

We must start with the woman's right to choose. A woman's right to choose an abortion is a fully developed—if contested—constitutional and moral right. A woman's right to choose an abortion is, most centrally, a right against the state: The state cannot tell a woman what to do with her body.

It is also, of course, a right against the fetus: The woman's right to choose is the right to terminate a pregnancy, particularly in the first trimester, above any right that might be asserted on behalf of the fetus.

But the pro-choice position has another valence too, one that *Danforth* and *Casey* spell out most specifically: It is the woman's right to terminate her pregnancy without regard for the desires or concerns of the man involved. The right was designed with a particular evil in view: that the state or a father would try to use coercive means to prevent a woman from seeking an abortion. That is the core of the right.

Still, the right has come to mean more. The woman's right to choose also seems to encompass her right to carry the fetus to term if she wants to, irrespective of the desire of the man or the state. Most people think this makes sense, and that this is a natural expression (if not a natural extension) of the woman's right to choose an abortion.

Nongendered Right to Procreative Choice

But it is worth pausing to notice that this extension creates thorny problems. Imagine the United States trying to adopt a family planning policy similar to the one in place in China, allowing families to have only two children.

What is wrong with such a policy? It seems clear that the policy is offensive to our moral and constitutional sensibilities. But would our first line of defense against such a policy derive from the woman's right to choose directly? I don't think so. Nor would it be enough to talk about a woman's right to bodily integrity, though that contributes a bit more toward explaining what is offensive about it.

If there is a right to decide for ourselves how many children to have, it is unlikely to inhere solely in women. We are offended by the idea of the China policy because it intrudes upon a more general right to procreative choice.

That right is not gendered; it includes both men and women. It is the right to make private decisions about how and when to procreate. Any effort to reject the China policy without accounting for the ways in which it infringes on men's rights would be inadequate.

This reasoning is of a piece with earlier Supreme Court decisions on the right to privacy, from which the right to choose an abortion was derived. Consider the Court's pronouncement in *Eisenstadt v. Baird* (1972): "If the right of privacy means anything, it is the right of the individual, married or single, to be free from unwarranted governmental intrusion into matters so fundamentally affecting a person as the decision whether to bear or beget a child."

Nowhere are women given especial focus in the right to privacy; men retain the right to procreate or not to procreate.

Men's Interests

That didn't last for long, of course; *Danforth* and *Casey* cemented the idea that, as *Danforth* put it, "We cannot hold that the state has the constitutional authority to give the spouse unilaterally the ability to prohibit the wife from terminating her pregnancy, when the state itself lacks that right."

Still, the Court was not totally dismissive of the man's rights in choosing whether to become a parent. For example, in *Casey*, the Court affirmed that a man has a "deep and proper concern and interest . . . in his wife's pregnancy and in the growth and development of the fetus she is carrying." And the Court rightfully appreciated that in well-functioning relationships, women would notify and consult with the father.

Yet, citing a long string of factual findings about domestic violence and enlisting a parade of horribles that would follow from giving the father more substantial rights in the fetus, the Court made clear that the woman's right to choose could not be qualified in any way by giving a man any say in the matter.

This may be fine as a matter of law and as a decision rule for when the parties disagree. But it also enables women to jump right to their veto power without including the man. And it also opens the door for women to cloak themselves with the sanctity of the legal right to choose—and not consider that men have very real interests in the termination of a fetus they are responsible for creating—and for which they will have to pay dearly, even if they took all necessary precautions to avoid a pregnancy.

In short, I wish to suggest that consensual sex does not carry with it—without further specification or clarification—

an abdication of the man's interest in and right to the privacy of his genetic material. It does not waive his right not to be a father against his will.

We can have a decision rule that the woman will get to choose if it comes down to that—but it is much harder to assert that a man abdicates any participatory rights he may have in the decision-making process.

A Man's Right to Choose Abortion

How can we give teeth to the man's right to choose an abortion—other than merely hoping that women will consult with their partners?

Should a man who tries in good faith to avoid a pregnancy have the legal right to force an abortion on a woman he accidentally impregnates who prefers to carry the fetus to term? No. A man should not be allowed to force a woman to undergo a traumatic surgical or pharmacological procedure to abort a fetus. The Court certainly got right that morality requires that women get a final say.

Yet although women get the final say, there are nonetheless ways for the law to ensure that men still have a voice in the matter. First, we can allow suits like that in Illinois to vindicate the right, allowing claims for intentional infliction of emotional distress when the woman has forced a man to become a parent against his will.

Second, we can relieve men of support payments if they can show that they did what they could to avoid becoming a father. If a man exercises due care to prevent pregnancy, a woman who nevertheless carries the child to term ought to bear the financial consequences of her decision.

We should remain deeply concerned about deadbeat dads—but those who really wanted an abortion of an accidental fetus shouldn't be stigmatized and penalized for not getting the ability to choose an abortion.

Finally, we can allow men and women to contract out of support payments if a woman, without the man's consent, insists on carrying an accidental pregnancy to term. This option, not available under current law, would allow the couple to agree that a man could give up all parental rights and responsibilities, perhaps in exchange for a one-time payment to the woman to assist with the costs of birth.

However we choose to vindicate the right through the legal system, a man is entitled to be heard on the question of whether to abort a fetus he helped to create. Ideally, the decision about what to do with an unwanted pregnancy should be a joint enterprise between man and woman. While women may hold the legal ace of spades—the ultimate right to choose and veto—men at least should be able to get their cards on the table.

"Although the Eisenstadt ruling dealt specifically with laws restricting the use of contraceptives to married couples, the language of the decision was broad enough to encompass efforts to have a child as well as to avoid having a child."

Eisenstadt Supports the Right of Homosexuals to Have Children

Charlene Gomes

Charlene Gomes is the senior program manager for law school advocacy and outreach at Equal Justice Works, a nonprofit organization that works to promote public service careers for lawyers.

In the following viewpoint, Gomes contends that the right to privacy in reproductive choices, identified by the Supreme Court in Eisenstadt v. Baird, *has special significance for the rights of homosexuals. Although* Eisenstadt *struck down state laws that restrict access to contraception by adults, Gomes claims that the general reasoning about the right to privacy in the case protects not only the right to avoid having children—by having access to contraception—but also the right to have children. Gays and lesbians, she argues, face many unreasonable barriers to parenthood, and being allowed to marry and have children are key steps in recognizing the equal civil rights of homosexuals.*

Charlene Gomes, "Partners as Parents: Challenges Faced by Gays Denied Marriage," *Humanist*, vol. 63, November/December 2003, pp. 14–19. Copyright © 2003 by the American Humanist Association. Reproduced by permission of the author.

If the right of privacy means anything, it is the right of the individual, married or single, to be free from unwarranted governmental intrusion into matters so fundamentally affecting a person as the decision whether to bear or beget a child.

—*Supreme Court Justice William Brennan,*
Eisenstadt v. Baird, 1972.

I had just read these words in my constitutional law class in 1997 when a coworker of mine shared with me his and his partner's struggles to have a child. They, together with a lesbian couple with whom they were close, had made numerous attempts at pregnancy "the old-fashioned way"—by tracking ovulation and inserting the sperm with a turkey baster—to no avail. They had recently begun to explore artificial insemination and were again frustrated to realize they would have to travel quite far from their Virginia home to get to a state where the procedure was legally available to them. A Virginia statute restricts the procedure to couples who are husband and wife. Numerous other states have similarly restrictive statutes. It seems that these laws aren't constitutional in light of the Supreme Court's 1972 decision in *Eisenstadt v. Baird.* Although the *Eisenstadt* ruling dealt specifically with laws restricting the use of contraceptives to married couples, the language of the decision was broad enough to encompass efforts to have a child as well as to avoid having a child.

The Debate About Marriage

In the past several years, issues regarding gay marriage and gay families have become a regular part of the national debate and, to a lesser extent, political debate. In 1996 Congress passed the Defense of Marriage Act (DOMA) in response to a Hawaii law that granted same-sex couples the right to marry (the law was later overturned by the Hawaii state legislature). Since then, thirty-seven states have passed their own DOMAs.

At the same time, it has become progressively easier for gay families to gain custody of biological children, conceive biological children through various fertilization methods and services, and adopt children. Yet President George W. Bush, many religious conservatives, and even some Democratic presidential hopefuls have reaffirmed their belief that marriage by definition applies only to unions between one man and one woman.

Given all the national rhetoric about the sanctity of marriage and the importance of raising children within a legally recognized relationship, one would assume that legislators would take note of the growing numbers of young children being raised by gay parents and get to work passing legislation legitimizing their parents' relationship. Yet nothing could be further from the truth. Despite Canada's recent move toward legalizing same-sex marriages, the United States continues to show every intention of fighting tooth and nail against this broadening of marriage laws, including a recently proposed constitutional amendment barring same-sex marriage. Unfortunately, the opposite mood has prevailed.

Gay and Lesbian Parents

Data from the 2000 U.S. census reveal that approximately one in three lesbian/bisexual couples and 22 percent of gay/bisexual couples are raising children. According to the National Gay and Lesbian Task Force (NGLTF), estimates of the total number of children with at least one gay or lesbian parent range from six million to fourteen million. Yet these numbers only track gays who were willing to self-report on the census; many remain unwilling to reveal their sexual orientation to the federal government, as the government offers them no protection from discrimination. Thus, the numbers certainly underestimate the true number of gays raising children. Married heterosexual couples with children comprise only 23 percent of U.S. households.

Gay or straight, not all parents raise children equally. Parenting ability relies on a complex and unquantifiable mix of skills and emotions. Love, patience, empathy, and respect, along with the ability to provide necessities and discipline without being abusive, are a mere sampling of points along the infinite parenting spectrum. It is curious—and telling—that current debate focuses on the legal ability of gays to marry rather than their actual ability to maintain life partnerships and to raise productive, well-adjusted children.

Even so, gay parents face unique barriers in their efforts to care and provide for their children. According to the NGLTF, privileges enjoyed by heterosexual married couples but denied to gay parents include: legal recognition of the parent-child relationship for children born during the relationship; recognition of parental status under the Family and Medical Leave Act; access to child support when the parental relationship ends; the right to petition for visitation and custody after the dissolution of a relationship; and (in some states) adoption and foster parenting.

Paths to Parenthood

Same-sex couples become parents in a variety of ways. Some have children from previous heterosexual relationships while others are adoptive or foster parents. Lesbians may become pregnant through donor insemination and gay male couples are turning more and more to surrogacy arrangements.

According to the NGLTF, donor insemination use among lesbian couples has increased since the 1980s. While insemination seems like an ideal solution, practical and legal barriers make it less so. Insemination is very expensive and results aren't always guaranteed. Insurance rarely covers these services—at least where lesbians are concerned—and clinical infertility hasn't been demonstrated. In addition, the majority of states have yet to address the issue of whether the sperm donor is the legal father of the child. This leaves the child's legal parentage to chance, opening the door for future legal problems. Also, the inability to prove paternity can be a stumbling block later on if one or both of the partners needs to be availed of public benefits.

Likewise, the NGLTF reports that the use of surrogacy among gay men has been on the rise in recent years. Unlike donor insemination, a generally accepted practice across the social and professional landscape, surrogacy is often considered controversial. Many states discourage the practice and two prohibit it outright. Other states prohibit payment to the surrogate mother. As with insemination, the law is unclear as to who are considered the legal parents of the offspring. Some states recognize the surrogate and her spouse while others attribute parentage to the couple contracting with the surrogate.

Adoption by Gays and Lesbians

Only Florida specifically prohibits individual lesbians and gay men or same-sex couples from adopting children. Mississippi only prohibits same-sex couples from adopting and some states, such as Utah, prioritize heterosexual married couples as adoptive and foster parents. Other states that don't make it a specific consideration in adoption determinations often take sexual orientation into account if raised in the course of the proceeding. Even so, many states allow gays to adopt as individuals and many—including California, Connecticut, the District of Columbia, Massachusetts, New Jersey, New York, and Vermont—now allow joint adoptions by same-sex couples.

What is truly harmful for children of gay parents is the lack of legal protection arising out of a failure to recognize same-sex marriage or to allow adoption by nonbiological life partners. The situation of nonbiological same-sex partners is most similar to that of stepparents in heterosexual marriages. Generally, if the noncustodial biological parent consents, stepparents may adopt the children. Yet, in the same situation, same-sex life partners usually require rigorous home visits and family studies. Most states have recognized that in some limited circumstances stepparents can adopt even without the noncustodial biological parent's consent, yet this doesn't hold for same-sex life partners.

The child suffers needlessly when the nonbiological partner is unable to establish a legal relationship, especially should the biological parent die or the relationship otherwise dissolve. The child isn't entitled to financial support or inheritance rights if there is no will. Lack of legal protections for the nonbiological partner include custody and visitation privileges, consent to emergency medical treatment, and permission to attend parent-teacher conferences.

Children with an adoptive stepparent enjoy other benefits not available to children living with a same-sex parent who is unable to adopt. Some state worker's compensation programs and the federal Social Security survivor benefit program now permit minor stepchildren living with and dependent upon a stepparent to receive benefits after the stepparent's death. Additionally, the Family and Medical Leave Act allows unpaid leave to care for a stepchild. Extending these benefits and protections to same-sex couples by legitimizing their relationships would ensure that the children of these couples will be treated equally with children of heterosexual married couples. The benefits of according these protections to all children easily outweigh the externalities imposed on third parties disapproving of homosexual relationships.

The landscape is somewhat different in cases of second-parent adoption, where one member of a same-sex couple is a biological parent and the nonbiological partner wishes also to become a legal parent. Stepparents in heterosexual marriages encounter little or no barriers when it comes to adopting the child of the biological parent. The law assumes that such an arrangement is in the child's best interests. Approximately twenty-five states allow same-sex second-parent adoptions but the adoptions are costly and littered with invasive and time-consuming procedures. Unlike heterosexual couples in the same situation, same-sex couples are subjected to numerous home visits and intensive social work assessments to determine the suitability of the adoption. . . .

Custody Issues

As challenging as it might sometimes be for same-sex couples to create a family, keeping the family together can be equally challenging. For gay and lesbian parents, custody disputes, by nature emotionally charged and often contentious, pose additional threats not faced by their heterosexual counterparts. Although the laws governing custody vary from state to state, two universal principles govern: that the court should consider the "best interests" of the child when determining custody and that there is a strong preference for placing the child with a natural parent as opposed to a third party. Courts considering custody disputes between two natural parents have generally followed one of three approaches for determining the fitness of gay and lesbian parents: the nexus approach, the nexus approach as a minor factor, and the per se approach.

The nexus approach is used by the majority of states. It asks the court to consider the causal connection between the conduct of the parent and any adverse effect on the child. The court inquires into the abilities of the parent rather than deeming the parent per se unfit based on sexual orientation. Of the three approaches, the nexus test is the most fact based, focusing on actual evidence of the child's best interests as opposed to stereotypes or presumptions about the parent. The parent's sexual orientation is only considered if harmful effects are proven. Currently, the District of Columbia is the only jurisdiction in which sexual orientation in and of itself cannot be a conclusive factor in custody and visitation matters.

Similarly, the nexus as a minor factor approach has led some courts to maintain that the parent's sexual orientation is merely one of many considerations in determining the best interests of the child. It differs from the strict nexus approach in that courts using nexus as a minor factor will automatically consider the parent's homosexuality in determining the best interests of the child.

The per se approach holds that the parent's homosexuality presents a refutable presumption that the parent is unfit. It rests on the notion that children of homosexual parents cannot possibly thrive because of social stigma, peer harassment, and the threat to their own "normal" heterosexual development. For the most part, even very conservative courts have shifted away from this approach in recent years. The per se rule isn't without support, however. Noted family law scholar Lynn Wardle of Brigham Young University would apply a refutable presumption to all cases involving a homosexual parent. Wardle would allow the heterosexual ex-spouse who has been denied custody to use a gay parent's new relationship as grounds for modifying the custody agreement and thus grant custody to the formerly noncustodial ex-spouse.

Unfortunately, the per se rule ultimately harms the child it seeks to protect by fueling power struggles between parents and undermining the state's (and the child's) interest in the finality and continuity of the custody agreement. The per se approach effectively eradicates the requirement for the party seeking to gain custody to show a change in circumstances that would serve the child's best interests.

In addition, courts often impose restrictions on divorcing parents that typically deny economic support (and sometimes custody) to parents who are cohabiting with a partner to whom they aren't married. These restrictions unfairly burden gay parents because they aren't legally able to marry their partners like heterosexual parents can, forcing them to choose between their children and their partner.

For the most part, gay parents today have a much easier time gaining custody of their children than they have in the recent past. Cases denying gay parents custody on factors other than actual fitness stand out as an area that generally receives little attention. . . .

The Importance of Marriage

Issues addressing the rights of homosexuals appear daily in the news. Debates abound about gays' right to marry, raise children, and hold a leadership role in public, private, and religious entities. The fact that these issues have come to the fore and are being publicly discussed says much about current attitudes regarding homosexuals as people. As with previous civil rights struggles, the road to full personhood under the law is long and hard but worth the journey.

Those who continue to oppose the right of homosexuals to marry and otherwise be free from discrimination in employment, housing, inheritance, family matters, and the countless other rights that many heterosexuals take for granted base their objections largely on religious grounds. Hiding behind the facade of morality they call upon "tradition" as their key witness for refusal to change. But tradition is a red herring attempting to disguise what is fundamentally a religious objection based on—as Bush so eloquently put it—the "sanctity of marriage," meaning a one-man/one-woman relationship for the purpose of creating and raising God's children.

But truth will ultimately trump tradition and the truth is that God is an optional party to a marriage in the United States. The real foundation of a marriage is having a legally recognized relationship between two people that affords them numerous benefits and protections, along with a handful of duties. While many couples choose to marry in a religious ceremony and plan to raise a family together, neither of these options is required and a couple is just as married if they have a civil ceremony and never have children. So how relevant is the "sanctity of marriage?" It is relevant only to those who choose to make it so within their own relationship.

Marriage is a wonderful and important societal institution. It signals to the community a dedicated respect, affection, and commitment to one's partner. It fosters a recognizable and familiar family structure that makes it possible to confer and enforce the legal benefits, protections, and responsibilities that go along with it. It provides stability and safety for one's partner and children in the event of tragedy or dissolution of the relationship. As such, it should be available to all people, regardless of their sexual orientation. Conception, adoption, and custody likewise shouldn't be compromised by an unfounded concern that exposure to homosexuality poses a danger to children. Rather, they should be based on the long-standing principle of the best interests of the child and a presumption in favor of the parents who choose to conceive, adopt, or otherwise raise the child.

As popular as ideas about the instability of gay families may be, they are based on fear and not on fact. Nearly all children are teased about something, whether it be the child's physical appearance, speech, ethnicity, race, religion, or economic status. Society will have its prejudices. In the 1984 case of *Palmore v. Sidoti*, the Supreme Court overturned a case refusing custody to a child's mother based on fear of harassment arising out of her interracial marriage, stating, "The Constitution cannot control such prejudices but neither can it tolerate them." Likewise, prejudice against gays' right to adopt is unconstitutional and should no longer be tolerated in the United States.

CHAPTER 3

Laws Banning Abortion Are Unconstitutional

Case Overview

Roe v. Wade (1973)

The issue of abortion is one of the most divisive issues ever to come before the U.S. Supreme Court. In *Roe v. Wade* (1973), the Court determined that the right of privacy under the Fourteenth Amendment protects a woman's right to have an abortion. Various issues about the right to abortion continue to come before the Court today.

A woman known as Jane Roe attempted to get an abortion in Texas, but a Texas law enacted in 1854 outlawed all abortions except to save the life of the pregnant woman. At the time of *Roe*, abortion was prohibited in the majority of states and severely restricted in all but four states. A Fifth Circuit Court ruling sided with Roe, striking down the Texas law as interfering with the fundamental right of women to choose whether to have children. The case was then appealed to the U.S. Supreme Court.

Harry A. Blackmun wrote the opinion for the 7-2 majority in favor of Roe, upholding the circuit court's decision. The Supreme Court determined that the right of privacy previously identified in cases such as *Griswold v. Connecticut* (1965) and *Eisenstadt v. Baird* (1972) also extended to a woman's right to terminate a pregnancy. Although the Court made clear that the right to abortion is fundamental, it determined that the right is not absolute. The Court held that the right to abortion varies by the trimester of pregnancy: In the first trimester, no restrictions can be made by the states on abortion; in the second trimester, the state may regulate abortion to protect the woman's health; and in the third and final trimester, states may completely restrict the right to abortion except in cases where the woman's life or health is at risk. The reasoning for allowing complete prohibition in the third trimester was the viability of the fetus—the fact that the fetus could likely live outside the womb beginning sometime in the third trimester.

The decision in *Roe* was controversial when it was made and continues to be politically divisive. Ever since *Roe*, states have enacted a variety of restrictive laws, testing the Court's parameters on abortion. The majority of the restrictions were struck down by the Court until *Planned Parenthood of Southeastern Pennsylvania v. Casey* (1992). In *Casey*, the Court rejected the trimester framework of *Roe*, allowing states to enact abortion restrictions that did not place an "undue burden" on a woman's right to abortion. The Court in *Casey* determined that a waiting period for abortion and consent requirements for minors did not constitute undue burdens, whereas a spousal notification requirement did. The Court will likely continue to hear cases regarding the constitutionality of restrictions on abortion, but the *Casey* decision further cemented the right to abortion in case precedent.

Majority Opinion: The Right to Privacy Includes a Right to Have an Abortion

Harry Blackmun

Harry Blackmun served as an associate justice of the Supreme Court from 1970 to 1994.

The following selection is excerpted from the majority opinion in the 1973 case Roe v. Wade, *the landmark decision wherein the Court determined that the constitutional right to privacy extends to the right of a woman to decide whether or not to have an abortion, agreeing with the lower court that a state ban on abortion violates the U.S. Constitution. Blackmun recounts the history of abortion laws in the United States, noting that the state laws at the time of* Roe *were more restrictive than they had been in the past. He considers and rejects three reasons offered for the existence of the Texas law criminalizing abortion. Discussing the right to privacy, Blackmun argues that a woman's decision about abortion is within this constitutionally protected zone of privacy. Rejecting the notion of the fetus as a person, Blackmun nonetheless notes that there is a compelling interest for the State to protect fetal life after the end of the second trimester and to protect the life of the mother after the end of the first trimester, thus allowing increasing restrictions in the second and third trimesters.*

Harry Blackmun, majority opinion, *Roe v. Wade*, U.S. Supreme Court, January 22, 1973.

The Texas statutes that concern us here are Arts. 1191–1194 and 1196 of the State's Penal Code. These make it a crime to "procure an abortion," as therein defined, or to attempt one, except with respect to "an abortion procured or attempted by medical advice for the purpose of saving the life of the mother." Similar statutes are in existence in a majority of the States. . . .

Jane Roe, a single woman who was residing in Dallas County, Texas, instituted this federal action in March 1970 against the District Attorney of the county. She sought a declaratory judgment that the Texas criminal abortion statutes were unconstitutional on their face, and an injunction restraining the defendant from enforcing the statutes. . . .

The principal thrust of appellant's attack on the Texas statutes is that they improperly invade a right, said to be possessed by the pregnant woman, to choose to terminate her pregnancy. Appellant would discover this right in the concept of personal "liberty" embodied in the Fourteenth Amendment's Due Process Clause; or in personal, marital, familial, and sexual privacy said to be protected by the Bill of Rights or its penumbras; or among those rights reserved to the people by the Ninth Amendment. Before addressing this claim, we feel it desirable briefly to survey, in several aspects, the history of abortion, for such insight as that history may afford us, and then to examine the state purposes and interests behind the criminal abortion laws.

The History of Abortion Laws

It perhaps is not generally appreciated that the restrictive criminal abortion laws in effect in a majority of States today are of relatively recent vintage. Those laws, generally proscribing abortion or its attempt at any time during pregnancy except when necessary to preserve the pregnant woman's life, are not of ancient or even of common law origin. Instead, they derive from statutory changes effected, for the most part, in the latter half of the 19th century. . . .

It is undisputed that, at common law, abortion performed before "quickening"—the first recognizable movement of the fetus *in utero* [in the uterus], appearing usually from the 16th to the 18th week of pregnancy—was not an indictable offense. The absence of a common law crime for pre-quickening abortion appears to have developed from a confluence of earlier philosophical, theological, and civil and canon law concepts of when life begins. These disciplines variously approached the question in terms of the point at which the embryo or fetus became "formed" or recognizably human, or in terms of when a "person" came into being, that is, infused with a "soul" or "animated." A loose consensus evolved in early English law that these events occurred at some point between conception and live birth. This was "mediate animation." Although Christian theology and the canon law came to fix the point of animation at 40 days for a male and 80 days for a female, a view that persisted until the 19th century, there was otherwise little agreement about the precise time of formation or animation. There was agreement, however, that, prior to this point, the fetus was to be regarded as part of the mother, and its destruction, therefore, was not homicide. Due to continued uncertainty about the precise time when animation occurred, to the lack of any empirical basis for the 40–80-day view, and perhaps to [medieval theologian Thomas] Aquinas' definition of movement as one of the two first principles of life, [English jurist Henry de] Bracton focused upon quickening as the critical point. The significance of quickening was echoed by later common law scholars, and found its way into the received common law in this country. . . .

In this country, the law in effect in all but a few States until mid-19th century was the preexisting English common law. Connecticut, the first State to enact abortion legislation, adopted in 1821 that part of Lord Ellenborough's Act [England's first criminal abortion statute, 1803] that related to a woman "quick with child." The death penalty was not imposed. Abortion before quickening was made a crime in that State only in 1860. In 1828, New York enacted legislation that, in two respects, was to serve as a model for early anti-abortion statutes. First, while barring destruction of an unquickened fetus as well as a quick fetus, it made the former only a misdemeanor, but the latter second-degree manslaughter. Second, it incorporated a concept of therapeutic abortion by providing that an abortion was excused if it "shall have been necessary to preserve the life of such mother, or shall have been advised by two physicians to be necessary for such purpose." By 1840, when Texas had received the common law, only eight American States had statutes dealing with abortion. It was not until after the War Between the States that legislation began generally to replace the common law. Most of these initial statutes dealt severely with abortion after quickening, but were lenient with it before quickening. Most punished attempts equally with completed abortions. While many statutes included the exception for an abortion thought by one or more physicians to be necessary to save the mother's life, that provision soon disappeared, and the typical law required that the procedure actually be necessary for that purpose. Gradually, in the middle and late 19th century, the quickening distinction disappeared from the statutory law of most States and the degree of the offense and the penalties were increased. By the end of the 1950's, a large majority of the jurisdictions banned abortion, however and whenever performed, unless done to save or preserve the life of the mother. The exceptions, Alabama and the District of Columbia, permitted abortion to preserve the mother's health. Three States permitted abortions that were not "unlawfully" performed or that were not "without lawful justification," leaving interpretation of those standards to the courts. In the past several years, however, a trend toward liberalization of abortion statutes has resulted in adoption, by about one-third of the States, of less stringent laws. . . .

It is thus apparent that, at common law, at the time of the adoption of our Constitution, and throughout the major portion of the 19th century, abortion was viewed with less disfavor than under most American statutes currently in effect. Phrasing it another way, a woman enjoyed a substantially broader right to terminate a pregnancy than she does in most States today. At least with respect to the early stage of pregnancy, and very possibly without such a limitation, the opportunity to make this choice was present in this country well into the 19th century. Even later, the law continued for some time to treat less punitively an abortion procured in early pregnancy. . . .

The Reasons for Abortion Laws

Three reasons have been advanced to explain historically the enactment of criminal abortion laws in the 19th century and to justify their continued existence.

It has been argued occasionally that these laws were the product of a Victorian social concern to discourage illicit sexual conduct. Texas, however, does not advance this justification in the present case, and it appears that no court or commentator has taken the argument seriously. . . .

A second reason is concerned with abortion as a medical procedure. When most criminal abortion laws were first enacted, the procedure was a hazardous one for the woman. This was particularly true prior to the development of antisepsis. Antiseptic techniques, of course, were based on discoveries by [English surgeon Joseph] Lister, [French chemist Louis] Pasteur, and others first announced in 1867, but were not generally accepted and employed until about the turn of the century. Abortion mortality was high. Even after 1900, and perhaps until as late as the development of antibiotics in the 1940's, standard modern techniques such as dilation and curettage were not nearly so safe as they are today. Thus, it has been argued that a State's real concern in enacting a criminal abortion law was to protect the pregnant woman, that is, to restrain her from submitting to a procedure that placed her life in serious jeopardy.

Modern medical techniques have altered this situation. Appellants and various *amici* [friends of the Court; nonlitigants who submit opinions or arguments in the case] refer to medical data indicating that abortion in early pregnancy, that is, prior to the end of the first trimester, although not without its risk, is now relatively safe. Mortality rates for women undergoing early abortions, where the procedure is legal, appear to be as low as or lower than the rates for normal childbirth. Consequently, any interest of the State in protecting the woman from an inherently hazardous procedure, except when it would be equally dangerous for her to forgo it, has largely disappeared. Of course, important state interests in the areas of health and medical standards do remain. The State has a legitimate interest in seeing to it that abortion, like any other medical procedure, is performed under circumstances that insure maximum safety for the patient. This interest obviously extends at least to the performing physician and his staff, to the facilities involved, to the availability of after-care, and to adequate provision for any complication or emergency that might arise. The prevalence of high mortality rates at illegal "abortion mills" strengthens, rather than weakens, the State's interest in regulating the conditions under which abortions are performed. Moreover, the risk to the woman increases as her pregnancy continues. Thus, the State retains a definite interest in protecting the woman's own health and safety when an abortion is proposed at a late stage of pregnancy.

The third reason is the State's interest—some phrase it in terms of duty—in protecting prenatal life. Some of the argument for this justification rests on the theory that a new human life is present from the moment of conception. The State's interest and general obligation to protect life then extends, it is argued, to prenatal life. Only when the life of the pregnant mother herself is at stake, balanced against the life she carries within her, should the interest of the embryo or fetus not prevail. Logically, of course, a legitimate state interest in this area need not stand or fail on acceptance of the belief that life begins at conception or at some other point prior to live birth. In assessing the State's interest, recognition may be given to the less rigid claim that as long as at least potential life is involved, the State may assert interests beyond the protection of the pregnant woman alone. . . .

The Right of Privacy

The Constitution does not explicitly mention any right of privacy. In a line of decisions, however, going back perhaps as far as *Union Pacific R. Co. v. Botsford* (1891), the Court has recognized that a right of personal privacy, or a guarantee of certain areas or zones of privacy, does exist under the Constitution. In varying contexts, the Court or individual Justices have, indeed, found at least the roots of that right in the First Amendment, in the Fourth and Fifth Amendments, in the penumbras of the Bill of Rights, in the Ninth Amendment, or in the concept of liberty guaranteed by the first section of the Fourteenth Amendment. These decisions make it clear that only personal rights that can be deemed "fundamental" or "implicit in the concept of ordered liberty," *Palko v. Connecticut* (1937), are included in this guarantee of personal privacy. They also make it clear that the right has some extension to activities relating to marriage, procreation, contraception, family relationships, and childrearing and education.

This right of privacy, whether it be founded in the Fourteenth Amendment's concept of personal liberty and restrictions upon state action, as we feel it is, or, as the District Court determined, in the Ninth Amendment's reservation of rights to the people, is broad enough to encompass a woman's decision whether or not to terminate her pregnancy. The detriment that the State would impose upon the pregnant woman by denying this choice altogether is apparent. Specific and direct harm medically diagnosable even in early pregnancy may be involved. Maternity, or additional offspring, may force upon the woman a distressful life and future. Psychological harm may be imminent. Mental and physical health may be taxed by child care. There is also the distress, for all concerned, associated with the unwanted child, and there is the problem of bringing a child into a family already unable, psychologically and otherwise, to care for it. In other cases, as in this one, the additional difficulties and continuing stigma of unwed motherhood may be involved. All these are factors the woman and her responsible physician necessarily will consider in consultation.

On the basis of elements such as these, appellant and some *amici* argue that the woman's right is absolute and that she is entitled to terminate her pregnancy at whatever time, in whatever way, and for whatever reason she alone chooses. With this we do not agree. Appellant's arguments that Texas either has no valid interest at all in regulating the abortion decision, or no interest strong enough to support any limitation upon the woman's sole determination, are unpersuasive. The Court's decisions recognizing a right of privacy also acknowledge that some state regulation in areas protected by that right is appropriate. As noted above, a State may properly assert important interests in safeguarding health, in maintaining medical standards, and in protecting potential life. At some point in pregnancy, these respective interests become sufficiently compelling to sustain regulation of the factors that govern the abortion decision. The privacy right involved, therefore, cannot be said to be absolute. In fact, it is not clear to us that the claim asserted by some *amici* that one has an unlimited right to do with one's body as one pleases bears a close relationship to the right of privacy previously articulated in the Court's decisions. The Court has refused to recognize an unlimited right of this kind in the past.

We, therefore, conclude that the right of personal privacy includes the abortion decision, but that this right is not unqualified, and must be considered against important state interests in regulation. . . .

The Fetus as a Person

The appellee and certain *amici* argue that the fetus is a "person" within the language and meaning of the Fourteenth Amendment. . . .

The Constitution does not define "person" in so many words. Section 1 of the Fourteenth Amendment contains three references to "person." The first, in defining "citizens," speaks of "persons born or naturalized in the United States." The word also appears both in the Due Process Clause and in the Equal Protection Clause. "Person" is used in other places in the Constitution. . . . But in nearly all these instances, the use of the word is such that it has application only post-natally. None indicates, with any assurance, that it has any possible pre-natal application.

All this, together with our observation, *supra* [above], that, throughout the major portion of the 19th century, prevailing legal abortion practices were far freer than they are today, persuades us that the word "person," as used in the Fourteenth Amendment, does not include the unborn. This is in accord with the results reached in those few cases where the issue has been squarely presented. . . .

A Compelling Interest in Protecting Life

Texas urges that, apart the Fourteenth Amendment, life begins at conception and is present throughout pregnancy, and that, therefore, the State has a compelling interest in protecting that life from and after conception. We need not resolve the difficult question of when life begins. When those trained in the respective disciplines of medicine, philosophy, and theology are unable to arrive at any consensus, the judiciary, at this point in the development of man's knowledge, is not in a position to speculate as to the answer. . . .

In view of all this, we do not agree that, by adopting one theory of life, Texas may override the rights of the pregnant woman that are at stake. We repeat, however, that the State does have an important and legitimate interest in preserving and protecting the health of the pregnant woman, whether she be a resident of the State or a nonresident who seeks medical consultation and treatment there, and that it has still *another* important and legitimate interest in protecting the potentiality of human life. These interests are separate and distinct. Each grows in substantiality as the woman approaches term and, at a point during pregnancy, each becomes "compelling."

With respect to the State's important and legitimate interest in the health of the mother, the "compelling" point, in the light of present medical knowledge, is at approximately the end of the first trimester. This is so because of the now-established medical fact . . . that, until the end of the first trimester mortality in abortion may be less than mortality in normal childbirth. It follows that, from and after this point, a State may regulate the abortion procedure to the extent that the regulation reasonably relates to the preservation and protection of maternal health. Examples of permissible state regulation in this area are requirements as to the qualifications of the person who is to perform the abortion; as to the licensure of that person; as to the facility in which the procedure is to be performed, that is, whether it must be a hospital or may be a clinic or some other place of less-than-hospital status; as to the licensing of the facility; and the like.

This means, on the other hand, that, for the period of pregnancy prior to this "compelling" point, the attending physician, in consultation with his patient, is free to determine, without regulation by the State, that, in his medical judgment, the patient's pregnancy should be terminated. If that decision is reached, the judgment may be effectuated by an abortion free of interference by the State.

With respect to the State's important and legitimate interest in potential life, the "compelling" point is at viability. This is so because the fetus then presumably has the capability of meaningful life outside the mother's womb. State regulation protective of fetal life after viability thus has both logical and biological justifications. If the State is interested in protecting fetal life after viability, it may go so far as to proscribe abortion during that period, except when it is necessary to preserve the life or health of the mother.

An Unconstitutional Law

Measured against these standards, Art. 1196 of the Texas Penal Code, in restricting legal abortions to those "procured or attempted by medical advice for the purpose of saving the life of the mother," sweeps too broadly. The statute makes no distinction between abortions performed early in pregnancy and those performed later, and it limits to a single reason, "saving" the mother's life, the legal justification for the procedure. The statute, therefore, cannot survive the constitutional attack made upon it here.

> "The drafters did not intend to have the
> Fourteenth Amendment withdraw from
> the States the power to legislate with
> respect to this matter."

Dissenting Opinion: No Constitutional Right to Have an Abortion Exists

William Rehnquist

William Rehnquist was a Supreme Court justice for thirty-three years (from 1972 to 2005), the last nineteen of which he served as chief justice. Rehnquist was considered a conservative member of the Court.

The following is Rehnquist's dissenting opinion in the 1973 case Roe v. Wade. *He disagrees with the Court's decision finding that the right to privacy protects a woman's right to have an abortion. Rehnquist agrees that a law restricting abortion when the mother's life is at stake would be unconstitutional, but he denies that the Constitution disallows states from making restrictions in any other situation. He argues that the Constitution gives states the right to make decisions about their compelling interests, and he decries the Court's review of state interests with respect to the Texas law restricting abortion. Rehnquist points to the fact that many states had laws restricting abortion when the Fourteenth Amendment was adopted in 1868, and its drafters did not question the validity of these state laws.*

William Rehnquist, dissenting opinion, *Roe v. Wade*, U.S. Supreme Court, January 22, 1973.

The Court's opinion brings to the decision of this troubling question both extensive historical fact and a wealth of legal scholarship. While the opinion thus commands my respect, I find myself nonetheless in fundamental disagreement with those parts of it that invalidate the Texas statute in question, and therefore dissent. . . .

The Right of Privacy

I have difficulty in concluding, as the Court does, that the right of "privacy" is involved in this case. Texas, by the statute here challenged, bars the performance of a medical abortion by a licensed physician on a plaintiff such as Roe. A transaction resulting in an operation such as this is not "private" in the ordinary usage of that word. Nor is the "privacy" that the Court finds here even a distant relative of the freedom from searches and seizures protected by the Fourth Amendment to the Constitution, which the Court has referred to as embodying a right to privacy.

If the Court means by the term "privacy" no more than that the claim of a person to be free from unwanted state regulation of consensual transactions may be a form of "liberty" protected by the Fourteenth Amendment, there is no doubt that similar claims have been upheld in our earlier decisions on the basis of that liberty. I agree with the statement of Mr. Justice [Potter] Stewart in his concurring opinion that the "liberty," against deprivation of which without due process the Fourteenth Amendment protects, embraces more than the rights found in the Bill of Rights. But that liberty is not guaranteed absolutely against deprivation, only against deprivation without due process of law. The test traditionally applied in the area of social and economic legislation is whether or not a law such as that challenged has a rational relation to a valid state objective. The Due Process Clause of the Fourteenth Amendment undoubtedly does place a limit, albeit a broad one, on legislative power to enact laws such as this. If the

Texas statute were to prohibit an abortion even where the mother's life is in jeopardy, I have little doubt that such a statute would lack a rational relation to a valid state objective under the test stated in *Williamson* [*v. Lee Optical Co.* (1955)]. But the Court's sweeping invalidation of any restrictions on abortion during the first trimester is impossible to justify under that standard, and the conscious weighing of competing factors that the Court's opinion apparently substitutes for the established test is far more appropriate to a legislative judgment than to a judicial one.

The Compelling State Interest Test

The Court eschews the history of the Fourteenth Amendment in its reliance on the "compelling state interest" test. But the Court adds a new wrinkle to this test by transposing it from the legal considerations associated with the Equal Protection Clause of the Fourteenth Amendment to this case arising under the Due Process Clause of the Fourteenth Amendment. Unless I misapprehend the consequences of this transplanting of the "compelling state interest test," the Court's opinion will accomplish the seemingly impossible feat of leaving this area of the law more confused than it found it. While the Court's opinion quotes from the dissent of Mr. Justice [Oliver Wendell] Holmes in *Lochner v. New York* (1905), the result it reaches is more closely attuned to the majority opinion of Mr. Justice [Rufus] Peckham in that case. As in *Lochner* and similar cases applying substantive due process standards to economic and social welfare legislation, the adoption of the compelling state interest standard will inevitably require this Court to examine the legislative policies and pass on the wisdom of these policies in the very process of deciding whether a particular state interest put forward may or may not be "compelling." The decision here to break pregnancy into three distinct terms and to outline the permissible restrictions the State may impose in each one, for example, partakes more of judicial legislation than it does of a determination of the intent of the drafters of the Fourteenth Amendment.

State Laws Restricting Abortion

The fact that a majority of the States reflecting, after all, the majority sentiment in those States, have had restrictions on abortions for at least a century is a strong indication, it seems to me, that the asserted right to an abortion is not "so rooted in the traditions and conscience of our people as to be ranked as fundamental" [*Snyder v. Massachusetts* (1934)]. Even today, when society's views on abortion are changing, the very existence of the debate is evidence that the "right" to an abortion is not so universally accepted as the appellant would have us believe.

To reach its result, the Court necessarily has had to find within the scope of the Fourteenth Amendment a right that was apparently completely unknown to the drafters of the Amendment. As early as 1821, the first state law dealing directly with abortion was enacted by the Connecticut Legislature. By the time of the adoption of the Fourteenth Amendment in 1868, there were at least 36 laws enacted by state or territorial legislatures limiting abortion. While many States have amended or updated their laws, 21 of the laws on the books in 1868 remain in effect today. Indeed, the Texas statute struck down today was, as the majority notes, first enacted in 1857, and "has remained substantially unchanged to the present time."

There apparently was no question concerning the validity of this provision or of any of the other state statutes when the Fourteenth Amendment was adopted. The only conclusion possible from this history is that the drafters did not intend to have the Fourteenth Amendment withdraw from the States the power to legislate with respect to this matter.

The Texas Statute

Even if one were to agree that the case that the Court decides were here, and that the enunciation of the substantive constitutional law in the Court's opinion were proper, the actual distortion of the case by the Court is still difficult to justify. The Texas statute is struck down *in toto* [in total], even though the Court apparently concedes that, at later periods of pregnancy Texas might impose these self-same statutory limitations on abortion. My understanding of past practice is that a statute found to be invalid as applied to a particular plaintiff, but not unconstitutional as a whole, is not simply "struck down" but is, instead, declared unconstitutional as applied to the fact situation before the Court.

For all of the foregoing reasons, I respectfully dissent.

> "There is no persuasive evidence that state abortion policies aimed, in one way or another, at talking women out of an abortion stop large numbers of women from having them."

Abortion Restrictions Since *Roe v. Wade* Have Not Significantly Reduced Abortions

Rachel Benson Gold

Rachel Benson Gold is director of policy analysis in the public policy division of the Guttmacher Institute, a nonprofit organization working to advance sexual and reproductive health in the United States and worldwide.

In the following viewpoint, Gold argues that state restrictions on abortion enacted since the 1973 decision in Roe v. Wade, *wherein the U.S. Supreme Court struck down state laws that categorically forbade abortion, have not been effective in reducing abortion. Gold claims that the antiabortion movement has been focused on deterring women from having abortions for decades. She points to recent Supreme Court cases that have encouraged states to create greater restrictions, leading to mandatory abortion counseling and mandatory ultrasound in some states. Gold argues that these policies have not been effective in reducing the number of abortions and concludes that efforts*

Rachel Benson Gold, "All That's Old Is New Again: The Long Campaign to Persuade Women to Forego Abortion," *Guttmacher Policy Review*, vol. 12, Spring 2009, pp. 19–22. Copyright © 2009 Guttmacher Institute. Reproduced by permission.

would be better used to keep women from getting pregnant rather than trying to prevent women who are already pregnant from getting abortions.

Just days after assuming office, prochoice President Barack Obama laid out his vision for a public policy agenda that would respond constructively to the ongoing national debate over abortion. "While this is a sensitive and often divisive issue," he argued, "no matter what our views, we are united in our determination to prevent unintended pregnancies, reduce the need for abortion, and support women and families in the choices they make." Within weeks, the administration announced an initiative to seek the advice of a wide range of individuals representing a diversity of views on how to move forward on this presumed common ground.

The Antiabortion Movement

Leading abortion opponents reacted quickly with alarm. Concerned Women for America President Wendy Wright, for one, requested a meeting with the White House, to protest how the administration's initiative was being framed. Calling concepts such as the need for abortion and unintended pregnancy "completely subjective," Wright argued instead for an explicit goal of reducing abortions. "What I think is important is [to] have measurable goals. . . . That's why it's important to look at the number of abortions."

Indeed, the organized antiabortion movement has never thrown its weight behind efforts to address abortion by helping women avoid unintended pregnancies in the first place. On the contrary, most national "profamily" and antiabortion organizations are either actively hostile to or, as in the case of the National Right to Life Committee, resolutely "neutral" on contraception and family planning service programs. Instead, they have worked to eliminate abortion altogether, by trying to ban the procedure outright. Failing that, or as a way of laying the groundwork, they have promoted a wide range of policies aimed at deterring as many women as possible from having an abortion. Many of these policies, at their heart, are premised on the notion that women who intend to have an abortion (and, to some extent, the public at large) do not fully understand what an abortion really is—and that, if they did, they would behave differently. As state Sen. Tony Fulton, sponsor of a legislative proposal in Nebraska to require women to be shown an ultrasound image of the fetus prior to having an abortion, recently argued, "If we can provide information to a mother who is in a desperate situation—information about what she's about to choose; information about the reality inside her womb—then this is going to reduce the number of abortions."

The Campaign to Dissuade Women

The campaign to dissuade women dates back decades. Outside facilities where abortions are performed, protesters for many years have confronted women with pictures of bloody fetuses, while "sidewalk counselors" implore women not to kill their babies. In the realm of public policy, a major initiative of long standing has been to enact mandatory "informed consent" policies; indeed, such policies have been addressed by the Supreme Court on three separate occasions. In its 1983 ruling [in *Akron v. Akron Center for Reproductive Health, Inc.*] on an ordinance passed by the city of Akron, Ohio, the Supreme Court struck down a law that required abortion providers to give women a litany of information the Court considered to be "designed not to inform the woman's consent but rather to persuade her to withhold it altogether." Nearly a decade later, however, a differently constituted Court revisited the issue in *Planned Parenthood of Southeastern Pennsylvania et. al., v. Casey* [1992], and allowed states to provide reformation under the aegis of informed consent, even if the stated purpose was "to persuade the woman to choose childbirth over abortion."

Most recently, in *Gonzales v. Carhart* [2007], the Court invited states to take a new look at the information women are required to receive prior to an abortion, specifically that regarding a description of "the way in which the fetus will be killed," on the grounds that "a necessary effect of [such a requirement] and the knowledge it conveys will be to encourage some women to carry the infant to full term."

State antiabortion activists widely accepted these judicial invitations. Currently, 33 states have some law or policy requiring the provision of specific information to women prior to having an abortion. According to a 2007 Guttmacher Institute analysis, the information required in 10 of these states generally comports with widely held principles of informed consent: a description of the procedure to be performed and information on the stage of the pregnancy. The laws in the remaining 23 states, however, are designed more to influence rather than inform the woman's decision. These laws, for example, often exaggerate the physical or mental health risks of abortion or include information on either fetal development or abortion procedures irrelevant to the abortions being sought by most women.

In 24 states, meanwhile, a "counseling" requirement is combined with a mandatory waiting period, a provision upheld by the Court in *Casey* on the premise that "important decisions will be more informed and deliberate if they follow some period of reflection." In most states, a woman may receive the mandated counseling information either over the telephone or via the Internet; in seven states, however, the law requires the counseling to be provided in-person at least 24 hours prior to the abortion, a provision that requires the woman to make two separate trips to the abortion facility.

Mandatory Abortion Counseling Materials

In 1985, portions of *The Silent Scream*, a lurid and medically inaccurate film portraying an ultrasound image of an abortion, were screened at a hearing held by a subcommittee of the Senate Judiciary Committee. The highly emotional narration depicts the image of the fetus as having its "wide mouth open in . . . the silent scream of a child threatened eminently with extinction." The film then goes on to urge that every woman considering an abortion should view the film before providing her consent.

A decade later, state antiabortion activists began working to have the same type of information as in *The Silent Scream* included in state-developed mandatory abortion counseling materials, but personalized to each abortion client's own fetus. Beginning in the mid-1990s, 13 states have adopted some provisions relating to ultrasound that stop short of requiring that the procedure be performed. These provisions range from requirements that all women seeking an abortion be given information about ultrasound technology to requirements that abortion providers offer women the opportunity to have the procedure and then view the image.

Some states have gone further by actually mandating that the procedure be performed for at least some women. Beginning with Arizona and Louisiana in 1999, five states currently require providers to perform an ultrasound on at least some women seeking an abortion and then offer them the option to view the image. Finally, in the most extreme example, Oklahoma adopted legislation in 2008 that actually requires not only that an ultrasound be performed prior to every abortion, but also that the physician review the image with the woman; the legislation explicitly mandates that, if she chooses, the woman be permitted to "avert her eyes." Implementation of the Oklahoma measure is enjoined pending legal action, while similar legislation was introduced in Alabama, Indiana, Kentucky, North Carolina, Rhode Island, Texas and Wyoming.

Finally, Colorado-based Focus on the Family in 2005 launched "Option Ultrasound," an initiative to provide ultrasound machines to 650 crisis pregnancy centers across the country, based on their belief that the technology "carr[ies] the potential to save a significant number of lives." As of March 2009, the group claims to have provided 430 grants for ultrasound machinery or training in 49 states.

Effectiveness of State Abortion Policies

Providing women information specifically geared to dissuading them from having an abortion is a perversion of medical ethics in general and the informed consent process in particular. But no matter how well-worn the tactic, it does not appear to be effective in its purported goal of materially reducing the number of procedures performed. In fact, there is no persuasive evidence that state abortion policies aimed, in one way or another, at talking women out of an abortion stop large numbers of women from having them. At most, there is some indication from the data that erecting substantial, direct roadblocks in the path of women seeing an abortion—such as denying Medicaid subsidies to poor women or requiring women to make two separate trips to a facility to receive in-person counseling, and then wait 24 hours before the abortion—may have that result.

The reasons women express for deciding to have an abortion, and the way they talk about how they made their decision, make it clear that they carefully consider the realities of their own lives and their ability, at that time, to be the kind of parent they want to be to their current and future children. For many women having an abortion, the issue of caring for dependents is not an abstract one, but a reflection of their current lives. Among such women, six in 10 are already a parent.

Lowering the Abortion Rate

For most women, the decision to end a pregnancy—even a very early pregnancy—is a complex and deliberative one. Moreover, all evidence indicates that women overwhelmingly make a final decision about abortion before they arrive at an abortion facility. Six in 10 women having an abortion say that they consulted with someone, most often their husband or partner, in making their decision. Women typically take 10 days between having a positive pregnancy test and trying to make an appointment for an abortion. And providers report that almost all women obtaining abortions are sure of their decision to terminate their pregnancy before they have even picked up the phone to make an appointment. This kind of carefully considered decision-making is unlikely to be swayed by inaccurate and emotionally laden attempts to persuade them otherwise.

In short, attempting to persuade women who are already pregnant and who do not want to be that they really would prefer to carry their pregnancies to term is an unrealistic way to have a substantial effect on the nation's abortion rate. The primary way to lower levels of abortions is to take aim at the proximate cause, unintended pregnancy. And the most effective ways to do that are to promote consistent use of effective contraception by all sexually active women and men who are not actively seeking pregnancy; support the development of better, more user-friendly contraceptive methods; expand access to family planning counseling and contraceptive services for those who cannot afford them on their own; and ensure that all people are provided the medically accurate, age-appropriate and comprehensive sex education they need to equip them to make and implement responsible decisions about their sexual behavior and their sexual health.

> *"The 1990s decline in the abortion rate ... had virtually nothing to do with policies enacted by President Clinton, and much to do with the dramatic increase in the number of states that were enacting pro-life laws."*

Abortion Restrictions Since *Roe v. Wade* Have Prevented Abortions

Michael New

Michael New is assistant professor at the University of Alabama and adjunct scholar at the Cato Institute.

In the following viewpoint, New argues that state restrictions on abortion—including funding restrictions, informed consent laws, and parental involvement laws—have helped to reduce the number of abortions in recent years. New claims that pro-life politicians are part of the reason that such restrictions were passed and, thus, electing pro-life politicians is critical to the goal of reducing abortions. New believes that it is important to overturn Roe v. Wade, *the Supreme Court decision finding state bans on abortion unconstitutional. He cautions against this being the sole goal of the pro-life movement, as a reversal of* Roe *would simply put the issue back to the states, which could decide whether or not to ban abortion completely.*

Michael New, "Pro-life Laws and Politicians Reduce Abortions Contrary to Pro-Obama Claims," LifeNews.com, October 27, 2008. Copyright © 2003-2009 LifeNews.com. All rights reserved. Reproduced by permission.

As Election Day [2008] approaches, the mainstream media is, as usual, showcasing self-identified "pro-lifers" who are supporting the Democratic Party's pro-abortion presidential nominee [Barack Obama]. In 2004, a number of media outlets cited an analysis by ethicist Glen Harold Stassen which claimed—wrongly—that the number of abortions had increased slightly since President [George W.] Bush's inauguration in 2001.

The *New York Times* published an op-ed by Dean Mark Roche of Notre Dame encouraging pro-life Catholics to vote for John Kerry. This year the story is similar. Former [Ronald] Reagan administration Assistant Attorney General Doug Kmiec and Duquesne University Law Professor Nicholas Cafardi, both of whom claim to be opponents of abortion, have received plenty of media attention for their support of Barack Obama.

The Success of Pro-Life Politicians

Their arguments are the same ones put forward in 2004. They have not improved with age.

Most of these authors attempt to make one of two points: either a) that there is little that elected officials can do to curb abortion through legislation, or b) that the pro-life movement has not reaped any real benefits from supporting candidates who oppose abortion. Voters should, therefore, they argue, place greater emphasis on other issues. However, an examination of the history of the pro-life movement and a careful analysis of abortion trends demonstrate that these arguments are deeply flawed. In fact, the success of pro-life political candidates has resulted in substantial reductions in the abortion rate.

For instance, the 1990s decline in the abortion rate—a decline that is eagerly touted by these Obama and Kerry supporters—had virtually nothing to do with policies enacted by President [Bill] Clinton, and much to do with the dramatic increase in the number of states that were enacting pro-life laws. The information below comes from [pro-choice organization] NARAL's *Who Decides*, an annual publication which provides information about abortion legislation:

- In 1992, virtually no states were enforcing informed-consent laws; by 2000, 27 states had informed-consent laws in effect.

- In 1992, no states had banned or restricted partial-birth abortion; by 2000, twelve states had bans or restrictions in effect.

- In 1992, only 20 states were enforcing parental-involvement statutes; by 2000, 32 states were enforcing these laws.

The Evidence of Effectiveness

Furthermore, there is plenty of evidence which suggests that these and other types of pro-life legislation have been effective at reducing the incidence of abortion.

There are a number of studies in peer reviewed academic journals that indicate that restrictions on public funding reduce abortion rates. In fact, there is close to a consensus on this subject among social scientists. I have conducted three studies which have examined state abortion data from almost every state for every year from 1985 to 1999. Each study finds that these state level public funding restrictions reduce the incidence of abortions by over 10 percent.

Informed consent laws require that women seeking abortions receive information about public and private sources of support for single mothers, health risks, and fetal development. Between 1992 and 2000, 27 states have enacted informed consent laws. Abortion data obtained from both the pro-abortion Alan Guttmacher Institute (AGI) and the officially neutral Centers for Disease Control (CDC) indicate that informed consent laws reduce the incidence of abortion. Furthermore, natural experiments which compare the effects of nullified laws to enacted laws have shown that nullified laws have no real effect on state abortion rates whereas enacted laws result in fewer abortions. This provides more evidence for the effectiveness of informed consent laws.

There exist at least 8 studies in peer reviewed academic journals—including one in *The New England Journal of Medicine*—which demonstrate that pro-life parental involvement laws reduce the in-state abortion rate for minors anywhere from 13 percent to 19 percent. Furthermore, a recent study I have conducted shows that more protective parental involvement laws—those that require parental consent and those that require the involvement of two parents—result in even larger decreases in abortion.

Case studies provide still more evidence of the effectiveness of state level pro-life legislation. Between 1992 and 2000 the overall abortion rate declined by 14 percent (among the 47 states reporting data both years). However, those states that were especially active in enacting pro-life legislation during the 1990s experienced even larger decreases in abortions.

Evidence from Four States

Mississippi has probably been more active than any other state in enacting pro-life legislation. During the 1990s the legislature enacted an informed consent law, the most protective parental involvement law in the country (one which requires the consent of both parents), a partial birth abortion ban, and a sweeping conscience clause allowing any medical professional to opt out of participating in an abortion. Abortion Rate Decline: 1992–2000: 52.07%

In the 1980s the Pennsylvania state legislature passed the Abortion Control Act, signed into law by the late Governor Robert P. Casey. It was one of the most comprehensive informed consent laws and included a parental consent law (It was the law the Supreme Court ruled on in its *Casey vs.*

Planned Parenthood decision in 1992). This law took effect sometime after the Supreme Court's decision. Abortion Rate Decline: 1992–2000: 23.50%

During the 1990s South Carolina passed a partial birth abortion ban, a parental consent law, an informed consent law, and an act regulating abortion clinics. Abortion Rate Decline 1992–2000: 33.57%

During the 1990s Michigan enacted a partial birth abortion ban, an informed consent law, a parental consent law, a ban on public funding, and abortion clinic regulations. Abortion rate decline 1992–2000: 21.39%

The Increase in Pro-Life Legislation

So what generated this increase in pro-life legislation? There are two primary factors and both directly result from the election of pro-life candidates. First, the Supreme Court nominees of Presidents [Ronald] Reagan and [George H.W.] Bush gave state level pro-life legislation greater deference in their *Casey v. Planned Parenthood* decision in 1992.

Many in the right-to-life movement were disappointed that the Supreme Court did not use *Casey* as an opportunity to overturn *Roe v. Wade* [1973]. However, in *Casey* the Supreme Court upheld as constitutionally permissible some of the policies contained in Pennsylvania's Abortion Control Act. As such, this decision afforded pro-life legislators at the state level more freedom to enact laws designed to protect the unborn.

Prior to *Casey*, the only laws that consistently withstood judicial scrutiny were parental-involvement laws and Medicaid-funding restrictions. After *Casey*, informed-consent laws were upheld. Informed-consent laws require women seeking abortions to receive information about fetal development, the health risks involved with obtaining an abortion, and public and private sources of support for single mothers. Furthermore, after *Casey* waiting periods and many state-level partial-birth-abortion bans were upheld as well.

Second, during the 1994 elections, Republicans won control of both chambers of the state legislature in eleven additional states. In many cases, Republicans maintained control over most of these legislatures through the end of the decade. Since Republicans at both the state and federal level tend to be more supportive of pro-life legislation, this made it easier for pro-lifers to enact protective legislation at the state level. Overall, there is no room for serious doubt that political victories by pro-life candidates have made a real difference.

The Reversal of *Roe*

In fairness, it should be noted that Kmiec, Cafardi, and others who are supporting Obama make one valid point. That is that the reversal of *Roe vs. Wade* will not be a panacea for the pro-life movement. Indeed, a reversal of *Roe* would simply give states the ability to restrict abortion. Not surprisingly, many states would not change their abortion policies at all if *Roe* were reversed.

However, the importance of reversing *Roe vs. Wade* should not be understated.

The damage done by *Roe vs. Wade* went beyond the legalization of abortion in all 50 states. *Roe* gave the idea of "abortion-rights" mainstream political credibility and shifted sexual and cultural mores in such a way as to make the enactment of pro-life laws more difficult. As such, a reversal of *Roe* would still do considerable good for the pro-life movement. It would further stigmatize abortion and remove judicial barriers from the enactment of pro-life legislation. However, pro-lifers need to be reminded that overturning *Roe* is only the first step. Indeed, enacting pro-life laws and changing the culture are battles that will engage the right-to-life movement for years to come.

During the past 35 years, the pro-life movement has made some real progress—progress that pro-lifers could at times do a better job of advertising. During the 1990s more states enacted parental-involvement laws, waiting periods, and informed-consent laws. More importantly, the number of abortions has fallen in 12 out of the past 14 years and the total number of abortions has declined by 24 percent since 1990. These gains are largely due to pro-life political victories at the federal level in the 1980s and at the state level in the 1990s, both of which have made it easier to pass pro-life legislation.

Furthermore, since the next President may have the opportunity to nominate as many as four justices to the Supreme Court, the right-to-life movement would be very well advised to stay the course in 2008.

> "Most Americans believe that abortion
> is wrong, but they also believe that it
> would be more immoral for the gov-
> ernment to interfere with ... private
> reproductive decisions."

The Majority of
Americans Do Not Want
Roe v. Wade Overturned

Ronald Bailey

Ronald Bailey is the science correspondent for Reason *magazine
and Reason.com, where he writes a weekly science and technology column.*

*In the following viewpoint, Bailey argues that politicians and
members of the Supreme Court should not try to overturn* Roe
v. Wade *(1973), the Supreme Court decision that provided
women with legal access to abortion in the first trimester. Bailey
claims that the number of abortions in recent years has gone
down (partly, he suggests, due to emergency contraception) and
has stabilized at its present level. Bailey considers the fact that
the American public still remains divided about abortion, even
years after* Roe. *Nonetheless, it would be a mistake to overturn*
Roe, *Bailey concludes, since most people want abortion to be an
option, even if they disagree with it.*

"If [Samuel] Alito replaces Justice Sandra Day O'Connor,
the Court will shift in a direction that jeopardizes the
fundamental values of freedom and privacy that a vast major-

Ronald Bailey, "*Roe v. Wade* Forever: Legalized Abortion's 33rd Anniversary," Reason
.com, January 20, 2006. Copyright © 2006 by Reason Foundation, 3415 S. Sepulveda
Blvd., Suite 400, Los Angeles, CA 90034, www.reason.com. Reproduced by permission.

ity of Americans want protected," declares a sample letter that NARAL Pro-Choice urges supporters to email to their senators asking them to block Judge Samuel Alito's confirmation to the U.S. Supreme Court. [In 2006 Alito was confirmed and sworn in.] The "freedom and privacy" that they fear Alito will put at risk is the high court's January 22, 1973 decision in *Roe v. Wade* that a woman has a relatively unfettered constitutional right to choose abortion during the first trimester of a pregnancy. Setting aside the still contested constitutional issue of the existence of a broad right to privacy (though if it doesn't exist, perhaps we should amend the Constitution to include it), how is abortion faring in the United States? Thirty years later, it's still a contentious muddle.

The Number of Abortions

First, the number of abortions is down since the early 1990s. According to the Centers for Disease Control and Prevention [CDC], in 1973, the year *Roe v. Wade* was decided, there were 615,831 abortions, which translates to an abortion ratio of 196 abortions per 1,000 live births and an abortion rate of 14 per 1,000 women between the ages of 15 and 44. The number of abortions peaked in 1990 at 1,429,247, yielding a ratio of 344 abortions per 1,000 live births and a rate of 24 per 1,000 women between the ages of 15 and 44. From that high, the number of abortions reported to the CDC had declined to 854,122 by 2002. (This number is artificially low, however. California, Alaska and New Hampshire stopped reporting their data to the CDC in 1998. In one year, the CDC estimated that women in California had 275,000 abortions, which would boost the U.S. total to more than 1 million.)

The Alan Guttmacher Institute compiles its own data from surveys of abortion providers. The institute's data indicate that there were about 800,000 abortions in 1973 and that the number doubled to around 1.6 million in 1990. Since then the number fell to just under 1.3 million in 2002. This implies that the CDC is missing data for about 450,000 abortions.

In any case, both data sets agree that the number of abortions in the United States declined during the 1990s and then essentially stabilized in the past few years.

Women with Unintended Pregnancies

Who gets abortions? Half of all pregnancies in the United States are unintended and about half of these unintended pregnancies are aborted. The CDC reports that 81 percent of the women who get abortions are unmarried and that 52 percent are under the age of 25. At current rates, one-third of American women will have had an abortion before they reach age 45. In *Roe v. Wade*, the Court declared that the state could limit fundamental rights only if the state had a "compelling interest" in doing so. Again setting aside the specific legal arguments, the Court further determined that states do not have such a compelling interest when it came to regulating abortions performed in the first trimester of pregnancy.

Thirty-three years later the vast majority of abortions occur in the court-sanctioned first trimester. Today, 60 percent of abortions occur before 8 weeks of gestation, and 88 percent of abortions are performed before the 13th week of gestation. (Interesting embryological note: at 8 weeks a fetus is 0.63 inches long and weighs 0.04 ounces; at 12 weeks, 2.13 inches and weighs less than half an ounce.) According to the CDC, fewer than 6 percent of abortions are done after 15 weeks of pregnancy (4 inches long and 2 and half ounces).

It is interesting to note that prescriptions for emergency contraception, the high dose birth control pills taken up to 72 hours after unprotected sex, have risen from 48,000 in 1998 when they were first approved to 310,000 in 2000. While usage of emergency contraception was increasing, the number of abortions dropped by about 35,000 between 1998 and 2000. This seems about right since only about 8 in 100 women who engage in unprotected sex during the second or third week of their cycle will get pregnant. Emergency contraception reduces this risk to 1 in 100.

American Public Opinion on Abortion

As the Alito hearing made plain, the fight over abortion still vexes our national conversation. The nonpartisan public opinion research organization, Public Agenda, points out that despite a generation of constant wrangling over abortion, American public opinion remains as divided as it was when *Roe v. Wade* was first decided. In 1975, a Gallup poll found that 54 percent thought abortion should be legal only under certain circumstances; 21 percent thought it should be legal in all circumstances; and 22 percent thought it should be illegal. In 2003, another Gallup poll saw these numbers shift to 57 percent; 24 percent; and 18 percent, respectively.

So what circumstances determine whether abortion should be legal or not for the mushy middle? According to polling data cited by Public Agenda, large majorities of Americans think that abortion should be legal to protect the life and health of the mother, or in cases of rape or incest. Smaller majorities believe that abortion should be legal to protect a mother's mental health, or when there is evidence that the developing child is mentally or physically impaired. Americans also favor various restrictions on abortion including laws requiring physicians to explain alternatives, waiting periods, and parental consent for women under age 18.

But when push comes to shove, 65 percent of Americans don't think that the government should interfere with a woman's access to abortion. (A poll this past summer [2005] found that 62 percent agreed with that sentiment.) Nearly 60 percent oppose a constitutional amendment that would ban abortion and 60 percent also think that *Roe v. Wade* should not be overturned by the Supreme Court.

Most Americans believe that abortion is wrong, but they also believe that it would be more immoral for the government to interfere with their fellow citizens' private reproductive decisions. If the Supreme Court dared to overturn *Roe v. Wade*, there would be political hell to pay. However, because most Americans remain ambiguously uncomfortable with abortion, our political institutions will fitfully continue to try to narrow the scope of the decision. Nevertheless, the central holding that a woman can choose abortion in the first three months of a pregnancy will not be overturned. Ultimately, our politicians realize that Americans want the *Roe v. Wade* escape hatch to be kept open just in case they or their loved ones have to make the hard decision to use it themselves.

CHAPTER 4

Laws Banning Birth Control for Minors Are Unconstitutional

Case Overview

Carey v. Population Services International (1977)

In *Carey v. Population Services International*, the Supreme Court determined that state laws attempting to limit minors' access to birth control are unconstitutional. Although the Court conceded that children's rights are not always the same as adults' rights, it argued that in this case the right to privacy regarding contraceptive choices was a right shared by minors. The right to privacy surrounding reproductive decisions to which the Court refers was first identified in *Griswold v. Connecticut* (1965), which protected the right of married persons to use birth control, and later in *Eisenstadt v. Baird* (1972), which protected the right of unmarried persons to use birth control.

A New York law at the time had made it a crime for anyone to sell birth control to minors under the age of sixteen, restricted contraceptive distribution for those of age to pharmacists, and forbade advertisement or display of contraception. A North Carolina mail-order company had been warned by New York officials that its distribution of contraceptives to New York residents violated the law. The mail order company filed suit against the State of New York, and the district court held that New York's law as it applied to nonprescription contraceptives was unconstitutional. The case was then appealed to the U.S. Supreme Court, where several other parties joined the mail-order company in disputing the law.

The Supreme Court affirmed the decision of the lower court, finding the law unconstitutional under the First and Fourteenth Amendments of the U.S. Constitution. First, the Court invalidated the portion of the law that restricted the distribution of nonprescription contraceptives to licensed pharmacists, finding it to pose too great a burden on the right of individuals to use birth control. Second, the Court concluded that the state's contraception age restriction unconstitutionally limited minors' right to privacy under the Fourteenth Amendment. Third, the Court concluded that the First Amendment protected the right to advertise and display contraception and that a total ban on such information was unconstitutional.

The Court's decision in *Carey* was not the first time the Court protected the reproductive rights of minors. Just a year earlier, in *Planned Parenthood of Central Missouri v. Danforth* (1976), the Court struck down a state law that required parental consent to obtain an abortion. Since *Danforth*, however, restrictions on minors' access to abortion have increasingly been upheld by the Supreme Court. In *Bellotti v. Baird* (1979), the Court struck down a law requiring minors to obtain informed consent from at least one parent or a court before receiving an abortion. However, the Court noted that a parental-consent restriction that allows a judicial bypass—an option for the minor to obtain permission from a court—would be constitutional. In fact, in *Planned Parenthood of Southeastern Pennsylvania v. Casey* (1992), the Court upheld such a law. In *H.L. v. Matheson* (1981), the Court upheld laws requiring a physician to notify parents of an immature minor before performing an abortion on that minor, reasoning that laws requiring only notification rather than consent were in the best interest of the minor. Many states and localities have enacted parental-consent or parental-notification restrictions on prescription birth control, and such laws may be challenged in the courts in the future.

> *"The constitutionality of a blanket pro-*
> *hibition of the distribution of contra-*
> *ceptives to minors is . . . foreclosed."*

Majority Opinion:
The Right to Privacy Protects
Contraception for Minors

William J. Brennan Jr.

William J. Brennan Jr. was a justice of the U.S. Supreme Court from 1956 to 1990. He was an outspoken liberal and is considered to be one of the more influential justices to have sat on the Court.

The following selection is excerpted from the majority opinion in the 1977 case of Carey v. Population Services International, *wherein the Supreme Court determined that state laws attempting to limit the access by minors to birth control are unconstitutional. A New York law at the time had restricted the sale and display of contraceptives in order to prevent access by minors under the age of sixteen. Coming to the same conclusion as the lower district court and affirming their decision, Brennan argues that the right to privacy with respect to reproductive issues—applied first in* Griswold v. Connecticut *(1965), and later in* Eisenstadt v. Baird *(1972) and* Roe v. Wade *(1973)—also supports the right of minors to have access to and information about contraceptives.*

Under New York Educ. Law § 6811(8) it is a crime (1) for any person to sell or distribute any contraceptive of any kind to a minor under the age of 16 years; (2) for anyone

William J. Brennan Jr., majority opinion, *Carey v. Population Services International*, U.S. Supreme Court, June 9, 1977.

other than a licensed pharmacist to distribute contraceptives to persons 16 or over; and (3) for anyone, including licensed pharmacists, to advertise or display contraceptives. A three-judge District Court for the Southern District of New York declared § 6811(8) unconstitutional in its entirety under the First and Fourteenth Amendments of the Federal Constitution insofar as it applies to nonprescription contraceptives, and enjoined its enforcement as so applied. . . .

The Right of Privacy

Although "[t]he Constitution does not explicitly mention any right of privacy," the Court has recognized that one aspect of the "liberty" protected by the Due Process Clause of the Fourteenth Amendment is "a right of personal privacy, or a guarantee of certain areas or zones of privacy" [*Roe v. Wade* (1973)]. . . . This right of personal privacy includes "the interest in independence in making certain kinds of important decisions" [*Whalen v. Roe* (1977)]. While the outer limits of this aspect of privacy have not been marked by the Court, it is clear that among the decisions that an individual may make without unjustified government interference are personal decisions

> relating to marriage, procreation, contraception, family relationships, and childrearing and education.

The decision whether or not to beget or bear a child is at the very heart of this cluster of constitutionally protected choices. That decision holds a particularly important place in the history of the right of privacy, a right first explicitly recognized in an opinion holding unconstitutional a statute prohibiting the use of contraceptives, *Griswold v. Connecticut* [1965], and most prominently vindicated in recent years in the contexts of contraception. This is understandable, for in a field that, by definition, concerns the most intimate of human activities and relationships, decisions whether to accomplish or to prevent conception are among the most private and sensitive.

If the right of privacy means anything, it is the right of the individual, married or single, to be free of unwarranted governmental intrusion into matters so fundamentally affecting a person as the decision whether to bear or beget a child. [*Eisenstadt v. Baird* (1972).]

That the constitutionally protected right of privacy extends to an individual's liberty to make choices regarding contraception does not, however, automatically invalidate every state regulation in this area. The business of manufacturing and selling contraceptives may be regulated in ways that do not infringe protected individual choices. And even a burdensome regulation may be validated by a sufficiently compelling state interest. In *Roe v. Wade*, for example, after determining that the "right of privacy . . . encompass[es] a woman's decision whether or not to terminate her pregnancy," we cautioned that the right is not absolute, and that certain state interests (in that case, "interests in safeguarding health, in maintaining medical standards, and in protecting potential life") may at some point "become sufficiently compelling to sustain regulation of the factors that govern the abortion decision." "Compelling" is of course the key word; where a decision as fundamental as that whether to bear or beget a child is involved, regulations imposing a burden on it may be justified only by compelling state interests, and must be narrowly drawn to express only those interests.

With these principles in mind, we turn to the question whether the District Court was correct in holding invalid the provisions of § 6811(8) as applied to the distribution of non-prescription contraceptives.

Right of Access to Contraceptives

We consider first the wider restriction on access to contraceptives created by § 6811(8)'s prohibition of the distribution of nonmedical contraceptives to adults except through licensed pharmacists.

Appellants argue that this Court has not accorded a "right of access to contraceptives" the status of a fundamental aspect of personal liberty. They emphasize that *Griswold v. Connecticut* struck down a state prohibition of the use of contraceptives, and so had no occasion to discuss laws "regulating their manufacture or sale." *Eisenstadt v. Baird* was decided under the Equal Protection Clause, holding that "whatever the rights of the individual to access to contraceptives may be, the rights must be the same for the unmarried and the married alike." Thus appellants argue that neither case should be treated as reflecting upon the State's power to limit or prohibit distribution of contraceptives to any persons, married or unmarried.

The fatal fallacy in this argument is that it overlooks the underlying premise of those decisions that the Constitution protects

> the right of the individual . . . to be free from unwarranted governmental intrusion into . . . the decision whether to bear or beget a child. [*Griswold*.]

Griswold did state that, by "forbidding the use of contraceptives, rather than regulating their manufacture or sale," the Connecticut statute there had "a maximum destructive impact" on privacy rights. This intrusion into "the sacred precincts of marital bedrooms" made that statute particularly "repulsive." But subsequent decisions have made clear that the constitutional protection of individual autonomy in matters of childbearing is not dependent on that element. *Eisenstadt v. Baird*, holding that the protection is not limited to married couples, characterized the protected right as the "decision whether to bear or beget a child." Similarly, *Roe v. Wade* held that the Constitution protects "a woman's *decision* whether or not to terminate her pregnancy." These decisions put *Griswold* in proper perspective. *Griswold* may no longer be read as holding only that a State may not prohibit a married couple's use of contraceptives. Read in light of its progeny, the teaching of *Griswold* is that the Constitution protects individual decisions in matters of childbearing from unjustified intrusion by the State.

The Importance of Access

Restrictions on the distribution of contraceptives clearly burden the freedom to make such decisions. A total prohibition against sale of contraceptives, for example, would intrude upon individual decisions in matters of procreation and contraception as harshly as a direct ban on their use. Indeed, in practice, a prohibition against all sales, since more easily and less offensively enforced, might have an even more devastating effect upon the freedom to choose contraception.

An instructive analogy is found in decisions after *Roe v. Wade* that held unconstitutional statutes that did not prohibit abortions outright but limited in a variety of ways a woman's access to them. The significance of these cases is that they establish that the same test must be applied to state regulations that burden an individual's right to decide to prevent conception or terminate pregnancy by substantially limiting access to the means of effectuating that decision as is applied to state statutes that prohibit the decision entirely. Both types of regulation

> may be justified only by a "compelling state interest" ...,
> and ... must be narrowly drawn to express only the legitimate state interests at stake [*Roe v. Wade.*]

This is so not because there is an independent fundamental "right of access to contraceptives," but because such access is essential to exercise of the constitutionally protected right of decision in matters of childbearing that is the underlying foundation of the holdings in *Griswold, Eisenstadt v. Baird*, and *Roe v. Wade*.

Limiting the distribution of nonprescription contraceptives to licensed pharmacists clearly imposes a significant burden on the right of the individuals to use contraceptives if they choose to do so. The burden is, of course, not as great as that under a total ban on distribution. Nevertheless, the restriction of distribution channels to a small fraction of the total number of possible retail outlets renders contraceptive devices considerably less accessible to the public, reduces the opportunity for privacy of selection and purchase, and lessens the possibility of price competition. . . .

State Power over Minors

The District Court also held unconstitutional, as applied to nonprescription contraceptives, the provision of § 6811(8) prohibiting the distribution of contraceptives to those under 16 years of age. Appellants contend that this provision of the statute is constitutionally permissible as a regulation of the morality of minors, in furtherance of the State's policy against promiscuous sexual intercourse among the young.

The question of the extent of state power to regulate conduct of minors not constitutionally regulable when committed by adults is a vexing one, perhaps not susceptible of precise answer. We have been reluctant to attempt to define "the totality of the relationship of the juvenile and the state" [*In re Gault*] (1967). Certain principles, however, have been recognized. "Minors, as well as adults, are protected by the Constitution, and possess constitutional rights" [*Planned Parenthood of Central Missouri v. Danforth* (1976)]. "[W]hatever may be their precise impact, neither the Fourteenth Amendment nor the Bill of Rights is for adults alone" [*In re Gault*]. On the other hand, we have held in a variety of contexts that "the power of the state to control the conduct of children reaches beyond the scope of its authority over adults" [*Prince v. Massachusetts* (1944)].

Of particular significance to the decision of this case, the right to privacy in connection with decisions affecting procreation extends to minors, as well as to adults. *Planned Parenthood of Central Missouri v. Danforth* held that a State

> may not impose a blanket provision ... requiring the consent of a parent or person *in loco parentis* [in the place of a parent] as a condition for abortion of an unmarried minor during the first 12 weeks of her pregnancy.

As in the case of the spousal consent requirement struck down in the same case, "the State does not have the constitutional authority to give a third party an absolute, and possibly arbitrary, veto," "'which the state itself is absolutely and totally prohibited from exercising.'" State restrictions inhibiting privacy rights of minors are valid only if they serve "any significant state interest ... that is not present in the case of an adult." *Planned Parenthood* found that no such interest justified a state requirement of parental consent.

Since the State may not impose a blanket prohibition, or even a blanket requirement of parental consent, on the choice of a minor to terminate her pregnancy, the constitutionality of a blanket prohibition of the distribution of contraceptives to minors is *a fortiori* [from the stronger argument] foreclosed. The State's interests in protection of the mental and physical health of the pregnant minor, and in protection of potential life are clearly more implicated by the abortion decision than by the decision to use a nonhazardous contraceptive.

The Deterrence Argument

Appellants argue, however, that significant state interests are served by restricting minors' access to contraceptives, because free availability to minors of contraceptives would lead to increased sexual activity among the young, in violation of the policy of New York to discourage such behavior. The argument is that minors' sexual activity may be deterred by increasing the hazards attendant on it. The same argument, however, would support a ban on abortions for minors, or indeed support a prohibition on abortions, or access to contraceptives, for the unmarried, whose sexual activity is also against the public policy of many State. Yet, in each of these areas, the Court has rejected the argument, noting in *Roe v. Wade* that "no court or commentator has taken the argument seriously." The reason for this unanimous rejection was stated in *Eisenstadt v. Baird*:

> It would be plainly unreasonable to assume that [the State] has prescribed pregnancy and the birth of an unwanted child [or the physical and psychological dangers of an abortion] as punishment for fornication.

We remain reluctant to attribute any such "scheme of values" to the State.

Moreover, there is substantial reason for doubt whether limiting access to contraceptives will, in fact, substantially discourage early sexual behavior. Appellants themselves conceded in the District Court that "there is no evidence that teenage extramarital sexual activity increases in proportion to the availability of contraceptives," and accordingly offered none, in the District Court or here. Appellees, on the other hand, cite a considerable body of evidence and opinion indicating that there is no such deterrent effect. Although we take judicial notice, as did the District Court, that with or without access to contraceptives, the incidence of sexual activity among minors is high, and the consequence of such activity are frequently devastating, the studies cited by appellees play no part in our decision. It is enough that we again confirm the principle that, when a State, as here, burdens the exercise of a fundamental right, its attempt to justify that burden as a rational means for the accomplishment of some significant state policy requires more than a bare assertion, based on a conceded complete absence of supporting evidence, that the burden is connected to such a policy. . . .

The Advertisement of Contraceptives

The District Court's holding that the prohibition of any "advertisement or display" of contraceptives is unconstitutional was clearly correct. Only last Term, *Virginia Pharmacy Bd. v. Virginia Citizens Consumer Council* (1976), held that a State may not "completely suppress the dissemination of concededly truthful information about entirely lawful activity," even when that information could be categorized as "commercial speech." Just as in that case, the statute challenged here seeks to suppress completely any information about the availability and price of contraceptives. Nor does the case present any question left open in *Virginia Pharmacy Bd.*; here, as there, there can be no contention that the regulation is "a mere time, place, and manner restriction," or that it prohibits only misleading or deceptive advertisements,

> that the transactions proposed in the forbidden advertisements are themselves illegal in any way.

Moreover, in addition to the "substantial individual and societal interests" in the free flow of commercial information enumerated in *Virginia Pharmacy Bd.*, the information suppressed by this statute "related to activity with which, at least in some respects, the State could not interfere."

Appellants contend that advertisements of contraceptive products would be offensive and embarrassing to those exposed to them, and that permitting them would legitimize sexual activity of young people. But these are classically not justifications validating the suppression of expression protected by the First Amendment. At least where obscenity is not involved, we have consistently held that the fact that protected speech may be offensive to some does not justify its suppression. As for the possible "legitimation" of illicit sexual behavior, whatever might be the case if the advertisements directly incited illicit sexual activity among the young, none of the advertisements in this record can even remotely be characterized as "directed to inciting or producing imminent lawless action and . . . likely to incite or produce such action" [*Cohen v. California* (1971)]. As for the possible "legitimation" of illicit sexual behavior, whatever might be the case if the advertisements directly incited illicit sexual activity among the young, none of the advertisements in this record can even remotely be characterized as "directed to inciting or producing imminent lawless action and . . . likely to incite or produce such action" [*Brandenburg v. Ohio* (1969)]. They merely state the availability of products and services that are not only entirely legal, but constitutionally protected. These arguments therefore do not justify the total suppression of advertising concerning contraceptives.

> "The Court's denial of a power so fun-
> damental to self-government must, in
> the long run, prove to be but a tempo-
> rary departure from a wise and hereto-
> fore settled course of adjudication to
> the contrary."

Dissenting Opinion: Minors Do Not Have a Constitutional Right to Birth Control

William Rehnquist

William Rehnquist was a Supreme Court justice from 1972 to 2005, the last nineteen of which he served as chief justice. Rehnquist was considered a conservative member of the Court.

The following is Rehnquist's dissenting opinion in the 1977 case of Carey v. Population Services International. *Rehnquist disagrees with the Court's decision, which found that the right to privacy protects minors' access to contraceptives and access to information about contraceptives. Noting that New York already allows abortion for minors (because of an earlier Supreme Court decision), Rehnquist finds it unreasonable that the state legislature not be able to craft a law restricting contraception, which it believes will deter sexual activity by teenagers. Rehnquist concludes that nothing in the U.S. Constitution supports the Court's decision to override the legislature of New York.*

Those who valiantly but vainly defended the heights of Bunker Hill in 1775 made it possible that men such as James Madison might later sit in the first Congress and draft

William Rehnquist, dissenting opinion, *Carey v. Population Services International*, U.S. Supreme Court, June 9, 1977.

the Bill of Rights to the Constitution. The post–Civil War Congresses which drafted the Civil War Amendments to the Constitution could not have accomplished their task without the blood of brave men on both sides which was shed at Shiloh, Gettysburg, and Cold Harbor. If those responsible for these Amendments, by feats of valor or efforts of draftsmanship, could have lived to know that their efforts had enshrined in the Constitution the right of commercial vendors of contraceptives to peddle them to unmarried minors through such means as window displays and vending machines located in the men's room of truck stops, notwithstanding the considered judgment of the New York Legislature to the contrary, it is not difficult to imagine their reaction.

The Court's Decision

I do not believe that the cases discussed in the Court's opinion require any such result, but to debate the Court's treatment of the question on a case-by-case basis would concede more validity to the result reached by the Court than I am willing to do. There comes a point when endless and ill-considered extension of principles originally formulated in quite different cases produces such an indefensible result that no logic chopping can possibly make the fallacy of the result more obvious. The Court here in effect holds that the First and Fourteenth Amendments not only guarantee full and free debate *before* a legislative judgment as to the moral dangers to which minors within the jurisdiction of the State should not be subjected, but goes further and absolutely prevents the representatives of the majority from carrying out such a policy *after* the issues have been fully aired.

No questions of religious belief, compelled allegiance to a secular creed, or decisions on the part of married couples as to procreation, are involved here. New York has simply decided that it wishes to discourage unmarried minors under 16 from having promiscuous sexual intercourse with one another. Even the Court would scarcely go so far as to say that this is not a subject with which the New York Legislature may properly concern itself.

That legislature has not chosen to deny to a pregnant woman, after the *fait accompli* [accomplished fact] of pregnancy, the one remedy which would enable her to terminate an unwanted pregnancy [abortion]. It has instead sought to deter the conduct which will produce such *faits accomplis*. The majority of New York's citizens are in effect told that however deeply they may be concerned about the problem of promiscuous sex and intercourse among unmarried teenagers, they may not adopt this means of dealing with it. The Court holds that New York may not use its police power to legislate in the interests of its concept of the public morality as it pertains to minors. The Court's denial of a power so fundamental to self-government must, in the long run, prove to be but a temporary departure from a wise and heretofore settled course of adjudication to the contrary. I would reverse the judgment of the District Court.

> *"The United States Constitution protects a minor's right to privacy in obtaining contraceptives."*

The Decision in *Carey* Supports the Right to Birth Control Without Parental Involvement

American Civil Liberties Union

The American Civil Liberties Union (ACLU) works in courts, legislatures, and communities to defend and preserve the individual rights and liberties guaranteed by the U.S. Constitution.

In the following viewpoint, the American Civil Liberties Union argues that proposals by state and federal lawmakers to require minors to obtain parental consent in order to have access to birth control are unconstitutional. The ACLU contends that research shows that the requiring of parental consent will not reduce teenage sexual activity and will increase teens' risk of acquiring sexually transmitted diseases. The ACLU argues that the Supreme Court's decision in Carey v. Population Services International, *which found laws banning minors' access to contraceptives unconstitutional, protects the rights of minors to have access to birth control without parental consent or notification. The ACLU also cites other public health policies that support minors' right to access confidential care.*

Today, in every state, sexually active teenagers can get contraceptives to protect themselves against unplanned pregnancies and sexually transmitted diseases—even if they can't talk about sex with their parents. But some state and federal lawmakers want to take away teens' ability to protect themselves. They want to prevent sexually active teenagers from getting birth control unless they first tell their parents.

These proposals would radically alter long-standing public health policy and put teenagers at risk. Studies show that preventing teens from getting contraceptives unless they tell a parent won't stop teenagers from having sex. It will just drive them away from the services they need to protect themselves, leading to higher rates of unintended pregnancies and sexually transmitted diseases (STDs), including HIV. For these reasons, the leading medical organizations oppose laws that would require teens to involve their parents before they can get contraception. Such laws would endanger teens' health and lives and violate their rights.

Research About Teen Behavior

Some people say that allowing teenagers to get contraceptives without first telling a parent encourages them to become sexually active and that, conversely, requiring teenagers to tell their parents before they get birth control would discourage sexual activity. But research about how teenagers behave flatly contradicts this theory. Teenagers don't become sexually active because they can go to a family planning provider and get contraceptives confidentially. In fact, on average, young women in the U.S. have been sexually active for 22 months before their first visit to a family planning provider. And studies show that making contraceptives available to teenagers does not increase sexual activity. Students in schools that make condoms available without requiring parental notification are *less* likely to have ever had sexual intercourse than students at schools that don't provide condoms confidentially. Moreover, in schools where condoms are readily available, those teens who do have sex are twice as likely as other students to have used a condom during their last sexual encounter.

The research thus shows that requiring teens to tell a parent before they can access contraceptive services doesn't reduce their sexual activity—it will just put their health and lives at risk. For example, a recent study published in the *Journal of the American Medical Association* looked at what sexually active teenage girls seeking services at family planning clinics in Wisconsin would do if they could not get prescription contraceptives unless the clinic notified their parents. The results are important for anyone who cares about teenagers' well-being:

- 47 percent of sexually active teenage girls said that they would stop accessing *all* reproductive health care services from the clinic if they couldn't get contraceptives without first telling their parents. Not only would these teenagers stop getting contraceptive services, they would also stop getting testing and treatment for STDs, including HIV;

- Another 12 percent would stop using some reproductive health care services or would delay testing or treatment for HIV or other STDs;

- This means that altogether 59 percent of sexually active teenage girls would stop or delay getting critical health care services; yet

- 99 percent of these teens—the ones who would stop or delay getting contraceptive services or STD testing and treatment—said they would continue having sex.

As this research shows, guarantees of confidentiality are one of the prime factors influencing whether a teenager will seek vital health services. In fact, in a nationwide study, the leading reason teenagers gave for not getting health care they knew they needed was concerns about confidentiality.

The Dangers of Preventing Access

Cutting off teenagers' access to contraceptives doesn't stop them from having sex, it just drives them out of doctors' offices. When teenagers don't visit family planning providers, not only do they forego contraceptive services, they also miss or dangerously postpone screening and treatment for STDs, routine gynecological exams, and other vital health care services. Teenagers are already a high risk population:

- Over half of all new HIV infections in the United States occur in adolescents.

- Every year three million U.S. teenagers contract a sexually transmitted disease. Left undetected and untreated, STDs can have lifelong consequences, including infertility.

- Teenage girls have the highest reported rates of chlamydia and gonorrhea.

- Close to 900,000 teenagers get pregnant each year. Four out of 10 girls get pregnant at least once before they turn 20.

If teenagers are prevented from getting contraceptives unless they involve a parent, these alarming numbers are likely to increase. A sexually active teen who does not use contraception has a 90 percent chance of getting pregnant within one year. In a single act of unprotected sex with an infected partner, a teenage girl has a 1 percent risk of acquiring HIV, a 30 percent risk of getting genital herpes, and a 50 percent chance of contracting gonorrhea.

Parental Notification and Consent

Medical experts caution that when teenagers cannot obtain contraceptives without involving a parent, they are less likely to protect themselves from unintended pregnancy and STDs. For this reason, the leading medical organizations, including the American Medical Association, the American Academy of Pediatrics, the American Academy of Family Physicians, the American College of Obstetricians and Gynecologists, the American Public Health Association, and the Society for Adolescent Medicine, among others, oppose laws that would require teens to involve a parent.

These groups have been vocal opponents of efforts to impose parental notification or consent requirements in federally funded programs. As these experts explained in a recent letter to Congress:

> "Most teens seeking services at [federally funded programs] are already sexually active. Mandating parental involvement is likely to discourage many teens from seeking family planning services, placing them at an increased risk for sexually transmitted diseases and unintended pregnancies. Studies indicate that one of the major causes of delay by adolescents in seeking contraception is fear of parental discovery and that many would avoid seeking services altogether if parental involvement were required."

The government cannot mandate healthy family communication. Federal law already requires health care providers in federally funded family planning clinics to encourage teenagers to talk to their parents about their health care decisions. Many teens, however, simply will not seek contraception if they cannot obtain it confidentially. Some justifiably fear that disclosure to their parents will lead to abandonment or abuse. Some simply have no caring and responsible parent to whom they can turn. Others live in families where sexuality is never openly discussed. As the New Jersey Supreme Court found, laws mandating parental involvement in teenagers' reproductive health care decisions "cannot transform a household with poor lines of communication into a paradigm of the perfect American family." Preventing teenagers from getting contraception unless they talk to a parent won't magically change these families; it will just result in teens having unprotected and unsafe sex.

Teens' Rights

The United States Constitution protects a minor's right to privacy in obtaining contraceptives. In *Carey v. Population Services International* [1977], the Supreme Court relied on minors' privacy rights to invalidate a New York law that prohibited the sale of condoms to adolescents under 16. The Court concluded that the "right to privacy in connection with decisions affecting procreation extends to minors as well as adults."

The Court held that the state interest in discouraging adolescents' sexual activity was not furthered by withholding from them the means to protect themselves. As Justice John Paul Stevens explained, to deny teenagers access to contraception in an effort to impress upon them the evils of underage sex is as irrational as if "a State decided to dramatize its disapproval of motorcycles by forbidding the use of safety helmets." The Constitution forbids this kind of "government-mandated harm."

Following the principles articulated in *Carey*, lower courts have invalidated parental involvement requirements for contraception. In *Planned Parenthood Association v. Matheson* [D. Utah 1983], for example, a federal district court recognized that teenagers' "'decisions whether to accomplish or prevent conception are among the most private and sensitive,'" and concluded that "the state may not impose a blanket parental notification requirement on minors seeking to exercise their constitutionally protected right to decide whether to bear or beget a child by using contraceptives."

In addition to minors' constitutional rights, two of the most important sources of federal family planning funds in the nation—Title X and Medicaid—mandate confidentiality for teenagers seeking contraceptive services in those programs. Federal courts have consistently ruled that parental consent and notification requirements impermissibly conflict with this mandate.

Moreover, virtually every state has passed laws permitting teenagers to obtain care for STDs without involving a parent and most have express legal provisions guaranteeing confidential access to contraceptives as well. Even in those states without express laws, teens still have a constitutional right to access confidential care. Forced parental involvement would represent a dangerous reversal of long-standing public health policies.

| "The right of parents to direct the up-
bringing and education of their children is a profound right."

Parental Rights Outweigh Minor Rights and Have Rightfully Expanded Since *Carey*

Colby M. May

Colby M. May is senior counsel of the American Center for Law and Justice, an organization that focuses on constitutional law, particularly religious freedom and freedom of speech.

In the following viewpoint, May contends that parental rights in the United States have been under attack for several decades. Citing recent court cases in the areas of education and medical decisions, he argues for greater recognition of the constitutional rights of parents to make decisions about the upbringing of their children. May claims that the reasoning within the Supreme Court's decision in Carey v. Population Services International, *which found laws banning minors' access to contraceptives to be unconstitutional, has been rightfully eroded in the last two decades. He argues that parental rights should continue to be expanded through legislation.*

The issue of parental rights in the face of government intervention is not a new one in this country; it has simply become a more burning issue as the intrusions have become more pronounced. As long ago as 1923, in a case called *Meyer*

Colby M. May, "Parental Rights: An Overview," *World & I*, vol. 12, May 1997, pp. 291–97. Copyright © 1997 News World Communications, Inc. Reproduced by permission.

v. Nebraska, the United States Supreme Court rejected the argument that the government's view of what led children to become patriotic and good citizens should prevail over the parents' view. The Court noted that in Plato's *Republic* the state was to rear children, and "no parent is to know his own child, nor any child his parent." The Court concluded, however, that the U.S. Constitution was founded upon precisely the opposite principle—that parents and not the government should bear responsibility for raising children:

> Although such measures have been deliberately approved by men of great genius, their ideas touching the relation between individual and State were wholly different from those upon which our institutions rest; and it hardly will be affirmed that any legislature could impose such restrictions upon the people of a state without doing violence to both letter and spirit of the Constitution.

Time and again, the Supreme Court has recognized the rights of parents to control the upbringing of their children—rights founded upon the First, Fifth, Ninth, and Fourteenth Amendments to the Constitution. As recently as 1990, the Supreme Court observed that, under the Fourteenth Amendment, the fundamental liberty interest of the parent to direct the education of the child is subject to strict scrutiny and cannot be overridden without showing a compelling state interest.

On the local level, however, the culture wars are raging around the rights of parents in the health, education, and moral upbringing of their children. Local government encroachment into areas traditionally the province of parents has resulted in a populist outcry and possible congressional intervention. Some relatively recent examples of current case law serve to illustrate trends in the ongoing battle between parents and the government.

The Children's Rights Movement

In the 1970s and early '80s the "children's rights" movement was in vogue. That line of sociological thinking led to the idea that children should have an equal say in their own upbringing. It was, perhaps, this underlying notion of childhood independence from parental authority and supervision that led the Washington State Supreme Court to find that parents could not punish a minor for involvement with sex and drugs. Parents had grounded their eighth-grade daughter because she engaged in premarital sexual activity and smoked marijuana. When the parents continued to have difficulty getting their daughter to obey, they asked for state assistance. While recognizing that the parents had imposed "reasonable rules which were reasonably enforced" [*In re Sumey* (Wash. 1980)] upon their daughter, the court nonetheless removed her from the home.

Social mores have guided much of the jurisprudence in the area of parental rights. In the 1960s the U.S. Supreme Court upheld a law banning the sale of pornographic magazines to children under seventeen years of age. In so doing the Court acknowledged that "[c]onstitutional interpretation has consistently recognized that the parents' claim to authority in their own household to direct the rearing of their children is basic in the structure of our society" [*Ginsberg v. New York* (1968)].

Thirty years later, Texas parents were denied the opportunity to see a mandatory assessment test that asked students personal questions concerning their family life, moral values, and religious beliefs. The parents sued and won, alleging that their responsibility for the upbringing and education of their children had been infringed. The Texas Education Agency on appeal asserted that "the right to direct the education and upbringing of your child is *not* a fundamental right." This position by the Texas Education Agency is not unique, but it is consistent with the view of many public educators that parental rights end at the schoolhouse gate.

The Content of Public Education

The battle concerning parental authority is most pronounced in the area of education. In the public school arena, recent state court rulings prevent parents from opting their children out of sexually explicit presentations that they find religiously or morally offensive. In a Massachusetts case, a presentation was given in which the instructor:

> 1) told the students that they were going to have a "group sexual experience with audience participation"; 2) used profane, lewd, and lascivious language to describe body parts and excretory functions; 3) advocated and approved oral sex, masturbation, homosexual sexual activity, and condom use during promiscuous premarital sex; 4) simulated masturbation; 5) characterized loose pants worn by one minor as "erection wear"; 6) referred to being in "deep sh—" after anal sex; 7) had a minor lick an oversized condom, after which the instructor had a female minor pull it over the male minor's entire head and blow it up: 8) encouraged a male minor to display his "orgasm face" for the camera; 9) informed a male minor that he was not having enough orgasms; 10) closely inspected a minor and told him he had a "nice butt"; and 11) made eighteen references to orgasms, six references to male genitals, and eight references to female genitals. [*Brown v. Hot, Sexy and Safer Productions, Inc.* (1st Cir. 1995).]

The 1st U.S. Circuit Court of Appeals found that no conscience-shocking activity had occurred at the public school assembly, because no physical intrusive contact had transpired. The court also found no constitutionally protected right for parents to opt their children out of the program. In a similar decision, the Massachusetts State Supreme Court found no constitutionally protected right for parents to object to public school condom distribution to their children. A contrary decision in New York found such a protected parental right.

The issue of character development, which has come to the fore in recent years, has engendered community service requirements as an integral part of public school education. A North Carolina school board recently required community service for graduation and told parents which specific extracurricular activities their children could engage in to meet the requirement. An Eagle Scout, however, in pursuit of his scouting achievements was not considered to be fulfilling a "true and selfless" community service, according to the school board.

The Issue of Home Schooling

One of the most hotly contested areas of education is home schooling and the question of how much oversight public authorities can have over parents teaching their children. In 1993, the Supreme Court of Michigan considered two home-schooling cases that were consolidated for oral arguments. At issue in the case was Michigan's requirement that all teachers be certified to teach, thus including home-schooling parents. In both cases, the children tested well within the state-specified boundaries for their educational peer groups.

In the case invoking a family that home-schooled because of religious convictions, the court found that the statute was unconstitutional because it violated the principles of religious freedom when combined with parental rights. In the second case, involving a family home schooling for nonreligious reasons, the parents lost. The rationale of the court was that the fundamental-rights analysis did not apply to a pure parental-rights claim without a religious component.

Parental Authority over Medical Procedures

It is axiomatic that parents have a duty to their children for their health and medical upkeep. The government, acting in its *parens patriae* (the country as parent) authority, can override a parent's wishes concerning his child's medical treatment. Most notable are those situations where the government has prevailed over parents' religiously based objections to such treatment as blood transfusions.

The issue of greatest concern for many parents has been their children's sexual education and involvement. A particularly contentious area has been parents' desire to intervene in a daughter's decision to have an abortion. The confluence of minors obtaining abortions and parental rights and responsibilities for medical care has led to a patchwork quilt of laws concerning medical procedures and parental authority. For example, in most states it is illegal for minors to get their ears pierced without parental consent. However, in many states government officials take the position that children's rights to serious medical procedures outweigh parental authority.

The Privacy Rights of Minors

Beginning with *Carey v. Population Services* (1977), the U.S. Supreme Court reviewed a New Jersey statute that made it a criminal offense to sell or distribute contraceptives to minors under the age of sixteen. The Court found this total prohibition to be in violation of the privacy right of minors who made the personal decision to use such devices. There was no majority opinion, however, on this particular issue. At that time, the justices declined to indicate a belief that parents have a constitutional right to be notified by a public facility when it distributes contraceptives.

Later cases wrestled with the issue of a minor's right to receive contraceptives without parental notification or consent. Generally, courts applying *Carey* found that there was no independent fundamental "right of access to contraceptives," but access to contraceptives was essential to exercise the constitutional right of decision in matters of childbearing. The underpinnings for the minor's right of private access to contraceptives remained grounded in the concept that the minor's right of privacy superseded the parents' right to direct their child's moral education.

In 1990, the Supreme Court began applying a different rationale to the issue of a minor's right of privacy in matters of childbearing, expressly overruling prior decisions on this point. In *Hodgson v. Minnesota* (1990), and *Ohio v. Akron Center for Reproductive Health* (1990), the Court upheld a statutory requirement of parental notification and/or consent prior to abortion if certain safeguards were met. The Court reiterated the basis for its transition on this issue in *Planned Parenthood v. Casey* [1992]:

> We have been over most of this ground before. Our cases establish, and we reaffirm today, that a State may require a minor seeking an abortion to obtain the consent of a parent or guardian, provided there is an adequate judicial bypass procedure. . . .

> Indeed, some of these provisions regarding informed consent have particular force with respect to minors: the waiting period for example may provide the parent or parents of a pregnant young woman the opportunity to consult with her in private, and to discuss the consequences of her decision in the context of the values and moral or religious principles of their family.

Denial of Parental Rights Claims

This idea that parents have a right in counseling and being involved with their children's sexual decisions and upbringing has often not been embraced by government authorities. For example, some Georgia parents found condoms in their daughters' room and subsequently discovered that their two teenage daughters had been driven to a county health facility during school hours where they received Pap smears, AIDS tests, condoms, and birth control pills. The parents were not informed of these medical procedures and did not consent to these activities. Moreover, when contacted by the parents for the results of their daughters' Pap smears and AIDS tests, both the school district and the county health facility refused to release the information, claiming patient confidentiality.

In 1944, the U.S. Supreme Court held that "[i]t is cardinal with us that the custody, care and nurture of the child reside first in the parents, whose primary function and freedom include preparation for obligations the state can neither supply nor hinder. And it is in recognition of this that these decisions have respected the private realm of family life which the state cannot enter [*Prince v. Massachusetts*]." The Massachusetts Supreme Court recently disagreed with this standard, however, ruling that parents had no claim in regulating or prohibiting the distribution of condoms within the Falmouth County public schools. The court found that a parental rights claim could not be made unless the schools coerced students in the distribution of condoms.

In the same vein, the 6th U.S. Circuit Court of Appeals affirmed a district court ruling that a Michigan couple did not have a fundamental parental right to prevent public school officials from forcing their third-grade son to undergo psychological counseling. The court held that the parents had no constitutionally protected right to object to the mental health treatments, or to even view the child's counseling records. The parents' solution to this dilemma of unwanted public school psychological counseling was to remove their son from the public school system and place him in a private school.

Proposals to Increase Parental Rights

In 1995 companion legislation was introduced by Sen. Charles Grassley (R-Iowa) and Rep. Steve Largent (R-Oklahoma) called the Parental Rights and Responsibilities Act (PRRA). The purpose of the act was to place the burden upon government officials, rather than parents, to prove the necessity of a governmental intrusion upon parental rights. Largent testified before a Senate subcommittee that

> [t]his protection is needed because the government is using its coercive force to dictate values, offend the religious and moral beliefs of families, and restrict the freedoms of families to live as they choose. State and lower Federal Court cases across the country illustrate that often times courts are using an inappropriate and unconstitutional standard in their consideration of parental rights claims.

The ACLU [American Civil Liberties Union] the National Education Association, and a host of other groups opposed this legislation, which expired with the end of the 104th Congress. Generally, the argument in opposition to the PRRA (and similar state proposals) is that it would unduly burden state and local authorities by forcing them to prove the necessity of decisions that impact families. In addition, they argue that the legislation would limit literature choices for youth, as well as have a negative impact on state child-abuse laws.

On the state level, efforts to strengthen parental rights have been made as proposals to amend state constitutions, as was the case in the November 1996 Colorado elections. While the measure was defeated, supporters have vowed to bring the measure up again, along with a more sophisticated "get out the message" effort to offset opposition by the large educational administrator and teacher unions. State laws codifying parental rights have also been proposed and are currently trader consideration.

The Parents Movement

At a time when more and more Americans believe the family is under severe pressure from government activities—from court rulings in Hawaii that hold denial of a marriage license to members of the same sex to be illegal discrimination, to programs that distribute condoms to eleven-year-old students but forbid the teaching of abstinence—is it any wonder the issue of parental rights has become so serious? While the "Parents Movement" may be just beginning, parental rights, like all personal liberty issues, have been with us as a society from our country's founding. As James Madison so compellingly wrote in *Federalist* 51:

> What is government itself but the greatest reflections on human nature? If men were angels, no government would be necessary. If angels were to govern men, neither external nor internal government would be necessary. In framing a government which is to be administered by men, over men, the great difficulty lies in this: You must first enable the government to control the governed; and in the next place oblige it to control itself.

The right of parents to direct the upbringing and education of their children is a profound right indeed. In today's America, with its numbing array of challenges, it seems sure this issue will be forced evermore to the front.

"Federal sponsorship of abstinence-only education impairs the constitutional rights minors enjoy with respect to their sexual health and procreation decisions."

Abstinence-Only Education Violates Minors' Rights Identified in *Carey*

Hazel Glenn Beh and Milton Diamond

Hazel Glenn Beh is professor of law at the William S. Richardson School of Law at the University of Hawaii–Manoa and co-director of the school's Health Law Policy Center. Milton Diamond is a professor and director of the Pacific Center for Sex and Society at the University of Hawaii–Manoa.

In the following viewpoint, Beh and Diamond argue that federal funding of abstinence-only education violates the rights of minors to have access to accurate information about sex. They contend that the justifications for abstinence-only education are analogous to New York State's justifications for the law at issue in Carey v. Population Services International, *which prevented minors' access to contraception. In* Carey, *the Supreme Court rejected New York's justifications by asserting minors' right to privacy with respect to procreation, thereby finding laws restricting access to contraception by minors to be unconstitutional. Beh and Diamond argue that the same reasoning applies to the government's attempt to keep information from minors, thereby proving abstinence-only education to be unconstitutional.*

Hazel Glenn Beh and Milton Diamond, "The Failure of Abstinence-Only Education: Minors Have a Right to Honest Talk About Sex," *Columbia Journal of Gender and Law,* vol. 15, Winter 2006, pp. 12–13, 44–58, 60–61. Copyright © 2006 *Columbia Journal of Gender and Law.* Reproduced by permission of the publisher and the authors.

The federal government spends over $170 million annually to subsidize states and community organizations that provide abstinence-only sex education to America's youth. This type of sex education is limited to teaching that a monogamous, marital, heterosexual relationship is the "expected standard of human activity" and that sex outside such a relationship will be physically and psychologically harmful. Abstinence-only education also advocates only one method to prevent disease and pregnancy, abstinence, and it offers no information concerning contraception and disease prevention except that all methods other than abstinence fail. As a result of its singular focus, the curricula not only pose significant problems with respect to ensuring minors' sexual health, but also ignore the needs of sexual minority youth altogether. . . .

Right to Comprehensive Sex Education

Not only is abstinence-only education harmful for minors, but it also infringes on their privacy and autonomy interests in sexual health and procreation. The current sex education debate is frequently portrayed as a dispute over what values to indoctrinate in American youth; however, this mischaracterizes the real controversy, which is first and foremost about what *information* minors should have, not what *values* they should be taught. When framed in this manner, the privacy and autonomy interests of minors to make their own decisions about their sexual health and procreation choices are implicated.

The issues surrounding adolescent sexuality raise nearly irreconcilable tensions between the adolescent, the parent, and the state, because each holds firmly established competing rights and interests. The constitutional infirmities related to federal funding of abstinence-only programs with overt religious messages have been explored elsewhere. However, religious entanglement issues are hardly the most harmful aspects of abstinence-only education. More detrimental is that these curricula endanger the health of minors and abridge the minors' constitutionally recognized privacy and autonomy interests related to sex. Once the federal government affirmatively provides or funds others to provide education about sexual health to minors, it owes minors a curriculum that will not harm them and that will respect, rather than impair, their constitutional rights. The omissions and deceptions prevalent within these unfounded curricula both prevent minors from making informed choices and expose them to potentially grave dangers.

When considering a minor's rights, parental rights and state interests are necessarily implicated as well; however, when either parents or the state are vested with power to make decisions for minors, they are empowered and obliged to act in the child's best interest. Parents are conferred the primary authority to inculcate moral and cultural values and to control the education of their children. This power, however, has traditionally been limited by co-existing duties to serve the interests of the child, and is grounded in the presumption that a parent's "natural bonds of affection lead parents to act in the best interests of children." [*Parham v. J.R.* (1979)].

Balancing Competing Interests and Rights

The state has competing interests aimed at protecting children and society; state interests in fact serve as a limitation on parental authority. In education, the state's interest has garnered a particular judicial respect, with the Supreme Court noting that "[p]roviding public schools ranks at the very apex of the function of a State" [*Wisconsin v. Yoder* (1972)]. Indeed, state interests in education cannot be underestimated, as the Court has characterized the public education of youth as essential to the nation's collective survival as a democratic society, stating that "[a] democratic society rests, for its continuance, upon the healthy, well-rounded growth of young people into full maturity as citizens, with all that implies" [*Prince v. Massachu-*

setts (1944)]. Like parental rights and "high duties," the state's role in education is characterized as both a state interest and an obligation to prepare minors for full participation in democratic society. Thus, both the rights of parents and the interests of the state are grounded in the presumption that their decisions are designed to protect and serve the needs of the child.

Children have their own rights that must be protected against the excesses of state or parental authority. However, as the Supreme Court has cautioned, in applying constitutional principles to children's rights, courts must demonstrate "sensitivity and flexibility to the special needs of parents and children" [*Bellotti v. Baird* (1979)]. Indeed, the Court has found that "the constitutional rights of children cannot be equated with those of adults" in light of "the peculiar vulnerability of children; their inability to make critical decisions in an informed, mature manner; and the importance of the parental role in child rearing." However, even when a child lacks a current capacity, a child's right to exercise self-determination in the future deserves protection and must be considered when possible.

The Issue of Sexuality

A particularly complex balancing of these competing interests and rights has occurred when addressing legal issues surrounding adolescent sexuality. This is because minors enjoy constitutional rights, albeit with some limitations, related to access to and decisionmaking about contraception and abortion, as well as other important health matters. When it comes to the issue of sexuality, the Supreme Court has explained that "the right to privacy in connection with decisions affecting procreation extends to minors as well as adults," and thus "[s]tate restrictions inhibiting privacy rights of minors are valid only if they serve 'any significant state interest . . . that is not present in the case of an adult'" [*Carey v. Population Services International* (1977)].

State laws frequently accord minors some relatively broad rights to make decisions related to sex. States, for example, often allow teenagers, without parental approval, access to testing and treatment for sexually transmitted diseases, prenatal care, contraception, permit decisionmaking concerning adoption and child-rearing, and prohibit forced sterilization. Moreover, while the age of consent has risen over the past 100 years, in the majority of states it remains below age eighteen. In short, even if some segments of society might prefer that minors delay sexual activity, state laws have accommodated the fact that the majority of adolescents are sexually active or will become so before majority, and recognize that decisionmaking related to sexuality should reside where possible with the individual.

Sex education thus represents a "perfect storm" of competing forces of parental rights, state interests, and children's rights. In conflicts regarding the education of children, court battles have traditionally focused on the clash between the parental right to raise children and the state's interest in preparing children for their role in a democratic society, with children's rights often taking a backseat in such disputes. As [legal expert] Barbara Bennett Woodhouse has observed, often in conflicts concerning children, courts have unfortunately often focused on how to weigh the parents' "private property" interest in the child against the state's interest in the child as a "public resource." The highly charged nature of the fight between parents and the state concerning sexual matters in particular makes it easy to neglect the distinct and significant rights of the minor in procreative and self-actualizing decisions.

Children's rights advocates argue that, with regard to issues concerning children, the conflict should not be viewed as principally one of balancing state interests against parental rights. Instead, when decisions are made about children, they should be child-centered and children's rights should not be subordinated to either state interests or parental rights. After all, the rights of both spring largely from their obligations to fulfill the needs of children. It is particularly compelling to change the focus in education cases from parental rights and state interests to the needs and rights of children because of the lifelong impact of educational choices on children. Of all the educational curriculum decisions that ought to be child-centered, none is more compellingly so than sex education due to the heightened privacy and autonomy interests the child enjoys both now and in his or her future.

Limits to Government Authority

When one puts the minor's interests first, the prerogative of the government to singularly teach abstinence, even if shorn of Establishment Clause [regarding freedom of religion] implications, rests on shaky constitutional grounds. These curricula impair the rights mature adolescents possess in matters concerning their own sexuality and exceed the government's right to promote its own message over others. By omitting or distorting information about sex and sexual health, including the efficacy of contraception, the consequences of abortion, and methods of disease acquisition and prevention, including specifically pertinent information for those youth that belong to sexual minorities, it is as though these programs have embarked on a scheme to prevent minors from making informed choices about rights the law has long accorded them. It is here that these programs cross the line of constitutionality.

There are well-established limits to the authority of the government to control adolescent procreative rights generally. As established in *Carey v. Population Services International*, "the right to privacy in connection with decisions affecting procreation extends to minors as well as to adults," and thus laws that impair adolescents' privacy rights are "valid only if they serve 'any significant state interest . . . that is not present in the case of an adult.'" *Carey*, decided over two decades ago, remains illustrative of the scope of a minor's procreative rights. The case considered the validity of a New York law that restricted the distribution of contraceptives to minors less than 16 years of age. New York argued that the law was intended to regulate "the morality of minors" and deter "promiscuous intercourse among the young," but the Court held that the law impermissibly burdened a minor's right to obtain contraception and, most notably, did not rationally serve to accomplish a significant state interest.

Failed Justifications

The justifications offered by New York in *Carey* for its restrictions on minors' access to contraception are remarkably similar to those which proponents of abstinence-only education offer today for restrictions on providing sex information to adolescents. New York claimed that access to contraception might promote adolescent sexual promiscuity; similarly, proponents of abstinence-only education claim that information about contraception might encourage licentious behavior. The *Carey* Court was astutely dubious of that justification in the absence of any proof:

> [T]here is substantial reason for doubt whether limiting access to contraceptives will in fact substantially discourage early sexual behavior. Appellants themselves conceded . . . that "there is no evidence that teenage extramarital sexual activity increases in proportion to the availability of contraceptives," and accordingly offered none. . . . Appellees, on the other hand, cite a considerable body of evidence and opinion indicating that there is no such deterrent effect. Although we take judicial notice, as did the District Court, that with or without access to contraceptives, the incidence of sexual activity among minors is high, and the consequences of such activity are frequently devastating, the studies cited by appellees play no part in our decision. It is enough that we again confirm the principle that when a State, as here, burdens the exercise of a fundamental right,

its attempt to justify that burden as a rational means for the accomplishment of some significant state policy requires more than a bare assertion, based on a conceded complete absence of supporting evidence, that the burden is connected to such a policy.

Just as New York could not rely on a bare assertion that access to contraception might encourage promiscuity, proponents of abstinence-only should not be able to depend on a vague and unsubstantiated claim that information about sex will encourage sexual activity.

New York also argued that, because minors could obtain contraceptives from physicians, the statute did not significantly burden a minor's privacy interests. The Court rejected the assertion, explaining that, even though the statute did not amount to a total prohibition on distribution of contraception to minors, it nevertheless constituted a significant burden on the right to decide whether to bear children. Finding "no medical necessity for imposing a medical limitation on the distribution of nonprescription contraceptives to minors," the court determined the law constituted a significant burden on a minor's right "to decide whether to bear children."

Abstinence-Only Education

Abstinence-only education impairs a minor's decisional interests just as significantly as New York's contraception ban did in *Carey*. Proponents of abstinence-only education defend the curricula, arguing in part that there are other avenues available for minors to obtain more comprehensive information. However, for some minors, there is no other avenue. In states that rely exclusively on money from federal abstinence-only education funds to teach sex education, a minor's constitutionally protected privacy interests in obtaining information about procreative choices may be significantly burdened because he or she may lack access to other outlets to obtain information.

However, even if one conceded both that the government has no obligation to fund any sex information and that all minors might obtain information elsewhere, such as through alternative school programs, family, friends, or health care providers, the ability of any minor who undergoes abstinence-only sex education to make informed decisions concerning sex is nonetheless significantly hampered both by what abstinence-only education teaches and what it omits. Since participants are erroneously instructed, for example, that abstinence is the only effective way to prevent disease and conception, and are not taught that contraception and condom use are effective methods of avoiding pregnancy and disease, they are burdened by erroneous instruction. Even where other sources of information are available, these students are unlikely to appreciate that they should and could seek more comprehensive sex instruction from a more reliable source. After all, a young person will very likely view a teacher working under the auspices of a program funded by the federal government as reliable and honest.

A Right to Accurate Information

Moreover, as in *Carey*, the state interest in current abstinence-only education policy is not justified as a rational means to accomplish a significant state policy. First, the goal of preparing minors to responsibly assume a proper position in democratic society, which underlies the state's interest in education, is not served by a singular focus on abstinence. Shaping values in education by withholding knowledge and information is antithetical to public education's purpose of preparing youth to make the weighty choices and decisions expected of America's citizenry. This is especially true given that [according to Mark G. Yudof,] "[o]ur social ideal is a democratic education, one that both prepares our young to choose for themselves and teaches them that their freedom to do so hinges on their respect and tolerance of the freedom of others to choose differently."

Second, the purpose of sex education is not merely to prepare adolescents to assume a future role as a sexual responsible adult in a democratic society. Biological and psychological realities dictate that sex education must educate minors to act responsibly now, and so teaching about sex cannot be postponed until adulthood. Sex education, because of its relationship to a minor's present health and reproduction rights, necessarily stands on a different footing than more mundane curricular choices, and for this reason the scale must tip in favor of the minor's right to comprehensive sex education. In matters of sexuality, mature adolescents have the capacity to engage in and make choices concerning sexual activities, and thus possess corresponding autonomy and privacy interests. Because adolescents are sexually mature at the time that sex education is presented to them, the minor's right to information is no less than that of an adult's.

State laws have vested in adolescents the right to make certain decisions regarding their sexual activities, and therefore the right to information logically inures to them. In the medical setting, a corollary of the right to consent is the right to receive adequate information to make an informed choice, which resides with the decision-maker. However, abstinence-only education only teaches minors to say "no," ignoring the concomitant right to knowledgably say "yes." Mature minors who are both physically and legally entitled to make sexual and reproductive decisions have a right to adequate information to make informed choices. Although sex education is conceptually different than medical treatment, it touches upon similarly private concerns related to autonomy. This is a crucial point, as adolescents are an underserved medical population, and thus formal sex education may provide the only forum through which teenagers might receive sexual health information.

Third, there can be no legitimate interest in affirmatively and deliberately misleading, deceiving, or depriving adolescents of health information when doing so might expose them to grave harms. Indeed, no one has offered a justification for delivering misleading, deceptive, and ineffective information about this important life topic. Further, requiring teachers to engage in such negative behavior forces educators to violate the educator's code of ethics. . . .

Federal sponsorship of abstinence-only education impairs the constitutional rights minors enjoy with respect to their sexual health and procreation decisions. Abstinence-only education's singular focus on abstinence, and its distortions concerning the effectiveness of methods of contraception and disease prevention, the risks associated with abortion, and the other consequences of sex misleads minors and compromises their ability and right to make informed health decisions. Indeed, recent studies suggest that abstinence curricula put minors at greater health risk than they would have been had they not taken any sex education course at all. Adolescents who have undergone abstinence-only education and who later engage in coital and non-coital activity, as most will prior to marriage, are ill-prepared to protect themselves; they may not use a condom because they do not know how or because they mistakenly believe that condoms are ineffective, may be unaware of the risks they experience when engaging in non-coital sexual activity as a strategy to remain "abstinent," and may be more vulnerable to adverse consequences of unprotected sex because they have not rehearsed and otherwise prepared for the contingency that they will not always be abstinent. Thus, by teaching abstinence as the only effective method to prevent disease and pregnancy, these curricula necessarily fail those adolescents who will hear, but not completely heed, that message. Therefore, federally funded abstinence-only education impairs a minor's ability to make informed choices and therefore impermissibly burdens his or her privacy and autonomy interests.

Organizations to Contact

The editors have compiled the following list of organizations concerned with the issues debated in this book. The descriptions are derived from materials provided by the organizations. All have publications or information available for interested readers. The list was compiled on the date of publication of the present volume; the information provided here may change. Be aware that many organizations take several weeks or longer to respond to inquiries, so allow as much time as possible.

American Center for Law and Justice (ACLJ)
PO Box 90555, Washington, DC   20090-0555
(800) 296-4529
Web site: www.aclj.org

The American Center for Law and Justice (ACLJ) is specifically dedicated to the ideal that religious freedom and freedom of speech are inalienable, God-given rights. The ACLJ has participated in numerous cases before the Supreme Court and federal and state courts regarding freedom of religion and freedom of speech. The ACLJ has numerous memos and position papers available on its Web site, including the memo, "Federal Healthcare Funding and Abortion."

American Civil Liberties Union (ACLU)
125 Broad St., 18th Fl., New York, NY   10004
(212) 549-2500
e-mail: infoaclu@aclu.org
Web site: www.aclu.org

The American Civil Liberties Union (ACLU) is a national organization that works to defend the rights guaranteed by the U.S. Constitution. The ACLU's Reproductive Freedom Project works to protect everyone's right to make informed decisions free from government interference about whether and when to become a parent. The ACLU publishes many reports, briefs, and news articles on its Web site, including "Reproductive Rights in the Courts: 2010."

Cato Institute

1000 Massachusetts Ave. NW, Washington, DC 20001-5403
(202) 842-0200 • fax: (202) 842-3490
Web site: www.cato.org

The Cato Institute is a libertarian public policy research foundation dedicated to limiting the role of government, protecting individual liberties, and promoting free markets. The Cato Institute commissions a variety of publications, including books, monographs, briefing papers, and other studies. Among its publications are the quarterly magazine *Regulation* and the bimonthly *Cato Policy Report*, that have contained articles such as "Limited Government versus the Supreme Court."

Center for Reproductive Rights

120 Wall St., New York, NY 10005
(917) 637-3600 • fax: (917) 637-3666
e-mail: info@reprorights.org
Web site: www.reproductiverights.org

The Center for Reproductive Rights is a global legal advocacy organization dedicated to reproductive rights. The Center for Reproductive Rights uses the law to advance reproductive freedom as a fundamental human right that all governments are legally obligated to protect, respect, and fulfill. The Center for Reproductive Rights publishes articles, reports, and briefing papers, among which is its signature publication, *Bringing Rights to Bear: Rights Within Marriage and the Family*.

Concerned Women for America (CWA)

1015 Fifteenth St. NW, Ste. 1100, Washington, DC 20005
(202) 488-7000 • fax: (202) 488-0806
Web site: www.cwfa.org

Concerned Women for America (CWA) is a public policy women's organization that has the goal of bringing biblical principles into all levels of public policy making. CWA focuses on promoting biblical values on six core issues—family, the sanctity of human life, education, pornography, religious liberty, and national sovereignty—through prayer, education, and social influence. Among the organization's brochures, fact sheets, and articles available on its Web site is "It's Time to Reject *Roe v. Wade* as Invincible Precedent."

Equal Rights Advocates (ERA)

180 Howard St., Ste. 300, San Francisco, CA   94105
(415) 621-0672 • fax: (415) 621-6744
e-mail: info@equalrights.org
Web site: www.equalrights.org

Equal Rights Advocates (ERA) works to protect and secure equal rights and economic opportunities for women and girls and fights for women's equality through litigation and advocacy. ERA produces several publications covering issues of equal opportunity, respectful and safe treatment, and work and family balance, including the Know Your Rights brochure titled "Family and Medical Leave/Pregnancy Discrimination."

Guttmacher Institute

125 Maiden Ln., 7th Fl., New York, NY   10038
(212) 248-1111 • fax: (212) 248-1951
Web site: www.guttmacher.org

The Guttmacher Institute works to advance sexual and reproductive health worldwide through an interrelated program of social science research, public education and policy analysis. The institute collects and analyzes scientific evidence to make a difference in policies, programs, and medical practice. Its monthly State Policies in Brief provides information on legislative and judicial actions affecting reproductive health, such as "Abortion Policy in the Absence of *Roe.*"

Human Life Foundation, Inc.

353 Lexington Ave., Ste. 802, New York, NY   10016
Web site: www.humanlifereview.com

The Human Life Foundation, Inc., is a nonprofit corporation with the goal of promoting alternatives to abortion. The organization works to promote alternatives to abortion through educational and charitable means. The foundation publishes the *Human Life Review*, a quarterly journal that focuses on abortion and other life issues.

NARAL Pro-Choice America

1156 Fifteenth St. NW, Ste. 700, Washington, DC   20005
(202) 973-3000 • fax: (202) 973-3096
Web site: www.naral.org

NARAL Pro-Choice America advocates for privacy and a woman's right to choose an abortion. NARAL Pro-Choice America works to elect pro-choice candidates, lobbies Congress to protect reproductive rights, and monitors state and federal activity in the courts related to reproductive rights. NARAL publishes numerous fact sheets, including "The Difference Between Emergency Contraception and Early Abortion Options."

National Right to Life Committee (NRLC)

512 Tenth St. NW, Washington, DC   20004
(202) 626-8800
e-mail: nrlc@nrlc.org
Web site: www.nrlc.org

The National Right to Life Committee (NRLC) was established to repeal the right to abortion after the decision in *Roe v. Wade* (1973). The NRLC works toward legislative reform at the national level to restrict abortion. NRLC publishes a monthly newspaper, the *National Right to Life News*.

Planned Parenthood Federation of America

434 W. Thirty-third St., New York, NY   10001
(212) 541-7800 • fax: (212) 245-1845
Web site: www.plannedparenthood.org

Planned Parenthood is a sexual and reproductive health-care provider and advocate. It works to improve women's health and safety, prevent unintended pregnancies, and advance the right and ability of individuals and families to make informed and responsible choices. On its Web site, Planned Parenthood offers information about birth control, as well as position papers, such as "Affordable Birth Control and Other Preventative Care."

For Further Research

Books

Howard Ball, *The Supreme Court in the Intimate Lives of Americans: Birth, Sex, Marriage, Childrearing, and Death*. New York: New York University Press, 2002.

Katherine T. Bartlett, *Gender and Law: Theory, Doctrine, Commentary*. 5th ed. New York: Aspen, 2009.

Barbara J. Berg, *Sexism in America: Alive, Well, and Ruining Our Future*. Chicago: Lawrence Hill Books, 2009.

Robert H. Bork, *The Tempting of America: The Political Seduction of the Law*. New York: Simon & Schuster, 1991.

Barry Friedman, *The Will of the People: How Public Opinion Has Influenced the Supreme Court and Shaped the Meaning of the Constitution*. New York: Farrar, Straus, and Giroux, 2009.

David J. Garrow, *Liberty and Sexuality: The Right to Privacy and the Making of* Roe v. Wade. Berkeley and Los Angeles: University of California Press, 1998.

Rochelle Gurstein, *The Repeal of Reticence: A History of America's Cultural and Legal Struggles over Free Speech, Obscenity, Sexual Liberation, and Modern Art*. New York: Hill and Wang, 1996.

John W. Johnson, Griswold v. Connecticut: *Birth Control and the Constitutional Right of Privacy*. Lawrence: University Press of Kansas, 2005.

Mark R. Levin, *Men in Black: How the Supreme Court Is Destroying America*. Washington, DC: Regnery, 2005.

Susan Moller Okin, *Justice, Gender, and the Family*. New York: Basic Books, 1989.

Jay Sekulow, *Witnessing Their Faith: Religious Influence on Supreme Court Justices*. Lanham, MD: Rowman & Littlefield, 2006.

Jeffrey Tobin, *The Nine: Inside the Secret World of the Supreme Court*. New York: Anchor Books, 2008.

David L. Tubbs, *Freedom's Orphans: Contemporary Liberalism and the Fate of American Children*. Princeton, NJ: Princeton University Press, 2007.

Joan Williams, *Unbending Gender: Why Family and Work Conflict and What to Do About It*. New York: Oxford University Press, 2000.

Bob Woodward and Scott Armstrong, *The Brethren: Inside the Supreme Court*. New York: Simon and Schuster, 1979.

Periodicals

Griswold v. Connecticut (1965)

Donna Brazile, "The Wrong Prescription," *Ms.*, Summer 2006.

Adrienne Burns, "Birth Control Rights Must Be Protected," *Atlanta Journal-Constitution*, June 7, 2005.

Connecticut Law Tribune, "*Griswold v. Connecticut*: 40 Years Later," July 11, 2005.

Cynthia Dailard, "What *Lawrence v. Texas* Says About the History and Future of Reproductive Rights," *Guttmacher Report on Public Policy*, October 2003.

Robert P. George and David L. Tubbs, "The Bad Decision That Started It All: *Griswold* at 40," *National Review*, July 18, 2005.

David Glenn, "Looking Back at a Landmark Court Decision in the Formal Development of a Right to Privacy," *Chronicle of Higher Education*, June 10, 2005.

Bradley P. Jacob, "*Griswold* and the Defense of Traditional Marriage," *North Dakota Law Review*, Fall 2007.

Courtney G. Joslin, "The Evolution of the American Family," *Human Rights*, Summer 2009.

Charlotte Low, "Privacy Decision Divides Scholars Two Decades Later," *Los Angeles Daily Journal*, June 10, 1985.

Andi Reardon, "*Griswold v. Connecticut*: Landmark Case Remembered," *New York Times*, May 28, 1989.

Carol Towarnicky, "Does Privacy Still Matter?" *Philadelphia Daily News*, August 23, 2005.

Lois Uttley, "An Inconceivable Argument," *Conscience*, Summer 2005.

Eisenstadt v. Baird (1972)

Gerard V. Bradley, "Stand and Fight: Don't Take Gay Marriage Lying Down," *National Review*, July 28, 2003.

Christopher Bruno, "A Right to Decide Not to Be a Legal Father," *George Washington Law Review*, November 2008.

Maria Doucettperry, "To Be Continued: A Look at Posthumous Reproduction as It Relates to Today's Military," *Army Lawyer*, May 2008.

Amitai Etzioni, "The Right to Privacy vs. the Common Good," *USA Today Magazine* , September 2000.

Journal of Contemporary Legal Issues, "Abortion: *Eisenstadt v. Baird*," Summer 2004.

Lynne Marie Kohm, "From *Eisenstadt* to Plan B: A Discussion of Conscientious Objections to Emergency Contraception," *William Mitchell Law Review*, Spring 2007.

Bernard G. Prusak, "How Should Judges Judge?" *Commonweal*, December 16, 2005.

Marc Spindelman, "The Honeymoon's Over," *Legal Times*, June 12, 2006.

Betsey Stevenson, "The Evolution of the American Family: An Economic Interpretation," *American Journal of Family Law*, Fall 2008.

Tonyaa Weathersbee, "When Women Had No Control over Their Bodies," *Jacksonville Florida Times Union*, January 30, 2006.

Roe v. Wade (1973)

Daniel Allott and Matt Bowman, "The Right of Conscience in the Age of Obama: It Can No Longer Be Taken for Granted," *American Spectator*, November 2009.

William F. Buckley Jr., "Questions of Life and Death," *National Review*, December 31, 2007.

Rebecca Dresser, "Protecting Women from Their Abortion Choices," *Hastings Center Report*, November/December 2007.

Dinesh D'Souza, "Sex, Lies, and Abortion: It's Time to Get to the Bottom of the Great National Tragedy," *Christianity Today*, September 2009.

Ruth Marcus, "Abortion's New Battleground," *Newsweek*, December 7, 2009.

Steven C. Moore, "A Tragic Inheritance: A Personal Perspective on the Abortion Debate," *America*, February 16, 2009.

Jon O'Brien, "Reducing the Need for Abortion: Honest Effort or Ideological Dodge?" *Conscience*, Spring 2009.

Star Parker and Gary Bauer, "A Dream Unfulfilled: *Roe v. Wade* Has Played a Big Role in the Devastation of the African-American Community," *Weekly Standard*, January 21, 2009.

Jeffrey Rosen, "The Day After *Roe*," *Atlantic*, June 2006.

Sam Schulman, "Honor Killing, American-Style: What Science and *Roe v. Wade* Made Possible Has Become Virtually Mandatory Among Our Self-Anointed Elites," *Weekly Standard*, April 13, 2009.

Jennifer Senior, "The Abortion Distortion: Just How Prochoice Is America, Really?" *New York*, December 7, 2009.

Michael E. Telzrow, "Before *Roe v. Wade*," *New American*, January 21, 2008.

Jeffrey Toobin, "Still Standing," *New Yorker*, November 28, 2005.

David Van Biema, "America Without *Roe v. Wade*," *Time*, September 25, 2008.

Jennifer N. Willcox, "Do Health Providers Have 'Right to Refuse'?" *Connecticut Law Tribune*, May 11, 2009.

Carey v. Population Services International (1977)

Jessica R. Arons, "Misconceived Laws: The Irrationality of Parental Involvement Requirements for Contraception," *William and Mary Law Review*, March 2000.

Elisabeth Frost, "Zero Privacy: Schools Are Violating Students' Fourteenth Amendment Right of Privacy Under the Guise of Enforcing Zero Tolerance Policies," *Washington Law Review*, 2006.

Harvard Law Review, "Constitutional Law—Right to Informational Privacy—District Court Grants Preliminary Injunction Against Enforcement of State Law Requiring Reporting of All Sexual Activity by Minors," December 2004.

Angela Patterson, "*Carey v. Population Services International*: Minors' Rights to Access Contraceptives," *Journal of Contemporary Legal Issues*, Summer 2004.

Internet Sources

Roe v. Wade (1973)

Deborah Kotz, "Should the Government Pay for Abortions?" *U.S. News & World Report*, December 8, 2008. www.usnews.com.

Carey v. Population Services International (1977)

Maggie Datiles, "Parental Involvement Laws for Abortion: Protecting Both Minors and Their Parents," *Culture of Life Foundation*, April 18, 2008. www.culture-of-life.org.

David L. Tubbs, "Supremely Inconsistent," *National Review*, June 30, 2005. www.nationalreview.com.

Index

C